Dimensions

of Discipline

rethinking practice in
secondary schools

David Gillborn
Jon Nixon
Jean Rudduck

London: HMSO

Department for Education
Sanctuary Buildings
Great Smith Street
London SW1P 3BT
071-925 5000

The name of the Department of Education and Science (DES) was changed to Department for Education (DFE) on 6 July 1992. However, the previous name is retained in this publication where appropriate.

The views expressed in this publication are those of the authors and do not necessarily reflect those of the Department for Education.

David Gillborn is Lecturer in Sociology of Education at the Institute of Education, University of London.

Jon Nixon is a Lecturer in the Division of Education, University of Sheffield.

Jean Ruddock is Professor of Education and Director, QQSE Research Group, Division of Education, University of Sheffield.

Contents

Authors' Notes   v

Preface   vii

1. Rethinking Discipline in Secondary Schools   1

2. Reconstructing Expectations   9

3. Working for Consistency   27

4. Developing Dialogue   45

5. Increasing Pupil Engagement   65

6. Building Shared Respect   89

7. Developing New Perspectives   109

8. References   119

Index   125

Authors' Notes

The Research Team

This book is based on research conducted between 1 April 1990 and 31 August 1991 and funded by the Department for Education.

The members of the research team were Dr David Gillborn, Dr Jon Nixon and Professor Jean Rudduck (who was also grant holder). Mrs Tina Cartwright and Mrs Brenda Finney provided secretarial support. The responsibility for fieldwork and for the initial drafting of the accounts was as follows: chapter 2 (JN); chapter 3 (DG); chapter 4 (JR); chapters 5 and 6 (DG). The final versions of these chapters are the result of intensive collaborative work by all three members of the team; chapters 1 and 7 are also the outcome of joint reflection and writing.

Acknowledgements

We should like to thank all the schools that agreed to participate in the research and all those individuals whom we interviewed. We would also like to acknowledge our debt to those people whom we consulted in the early stages of the project as the research was beginning to take shape. Finally, we would like to express our gratitude to the members of the Steering Committee – Roy Atkinson (Director of Education, Northamptonshire), Elizabeth Jones (HMI) and Tony Wilshaw (DFE) – for their advice and support and, in particular, for some useful and informative discussions.

Clearance

The accounts presented in chapters 2 to 6 have been discussed with the heads of the five schools, with any link persons designated by the schools, and with other teachers who were closely involved with the research. Throughout the report, reflecting our agreement with the people we worked with, we have made every effort to anonymise places, schools and individuals.

Terminology

For the sake of uniformity of style, we have standardised certain terms which in fact varied across schools. We use the term 'black' to denote people of both Afro-Caribbean and South Asian ethnic origin; and we follow the majority practice in the five schools and use the word 'pupil' rather than 'student'.

Preface

The schools that we worked with on this study were all invited to participate on the basis of their efforts to develop positive approaches to 'discipline' in teaching contexts that were not easy. In each case staff were engaged in re-thinking the idea of discipline as a unifying and constructive focus for their work with pupils – and with parents and the community. Common to each school setting was a concern for what we call *the dimensions of discipline* – encouraging high expectations; ensuring engagement in learning; using dialogue as a way of building shared understanding and a mutuality of trust; building relationships on respect; and being watchful that values and practices were coherent and consistent. At the same time, each school – reflecting the particularity of its circumstances – was giving priority to one or two of these dimensions.

We have identified a series of questions which relate to these dimensions and which are central to the idea of discipline as something that links the structures, relationships and ways of thinking that support learning in schools. Schools are all very different in terms of the pattern of problems and possibilities that they are balancing and we hope that the following questions will help them to rethink their own approach to discipline and provide them with a useful way into the studies that form the basis of this report. (The questions are presented more fully in chapter 7.)

Perspectives on Whole-school Organisation

Does the school have a sense of itself? What does it stand for and against?

Are staff moving towards an agreed set of values?

Are both staff and pupils confident in themselves and their purposes?

Are there structures and occasions which enable pupils and their parents to think about and discuss the school's purposes and practices?

Is there a clear code of conduct, which is understood to apply to teachers as well as to pupils?

Is there an orderly and 'safe' environment in the school?

What sources of support are there for those, both teachers and pupils, who feel 'unsafe'?

Perspectives on Pupils' Capacity for Learning

What sense do pupils have of their own achievements, educational needs and possible futures?

Are pupils helped to understand their own progress and are they involved in the assessment of their own work?

What opportunity is there for pupils to think through, with their teachers, the setting of tasks and the planning of appropriate personal targets?

What sense do pupils have of how their learning experiences 'add up' and achieve coherence?

Do pupils know what to do – and is there someone they feel they can talk to – if they experience a sense of failure or lack of direction in their work?

What messages does the school communicate about the worth of different individuals, groups and cultures?

1 Rethinking Discipline in Secondary Schools

We start with a word whose meaning we think we can understand ...
and begin to investigate the things which it designates. We always
find that it changes its meaning in the course of the investigation, and
sometimes we have to invent new words for the things we discover.

(Haldane, 1985; cited in Keddy, 1989)

In this book we start with a word – discipline – which in many people's
minds is associated with a particular set of meanings and practices.
Through a series of accounts of work in secondary schools we show how
these meanings and practices are being rethought in ways that reflect the
different contexts and histories of the schools, but also in ways that reflect
new concerns and new ways of looking at pupils and learning.

The research reported in this book is rooted in the daily reality of
teaching and learning in urban schools. This is not to say that the issues
which we analyse are of concern only to urban schools. By looking at the
ways in which these schools have begun to rethink the demands upon
them we hope to highlight key issues which have relevance for all schools
– but which also make sense even in some of the toughest locations.

Elton and after

Schools have probably always had to face behaviours – in the classroom,
in the corridor, in the hall, in the playground – which conflict with the offi-
cial *mores* of the institution. During the late 1980s, however, popular
images of state education in England and Wales frequently presented a
picture of serious, and worsening, violence and disruption. Using head-
lines such as 'National Chaos in the Classroom', the media played a significant part in constructing the view that there was a crisis of discipline in
state schools (see Docking, 1989, pp. 10–12). Growing public concern was
one of the factors that led Kenneth Baker, then Secretary of State for

1

Education, to establish, in March 1988, a Committee of Enquiry, chaired by Lord Elton.

With the publication of the Committee's Report, in March 1989, the media turned their attention to the finding that physical violence was in fact relatively rare in schools in England and Wales and that teachers did 'not see attacks as their main problem' (DES, 1989, p. 11).

Interestingly, this finding confirmed a review (see Docking, 1989, p. 13) of earlier research which had suggested that 'the daily stress-inducing problems that confront most teachers are more to do with fairly trivial but regular incidents of misbehaviour ... than with serious offences such as violence and verbal abuse'. A similar conclusion was reached in the independent research which the Elton Committee commissioned and which was presented as an appendix to the Committee's Report (Gray and Sime (1989); Gillborn, Nixon and Rudduck, 1989, pp. 215–77).

Violent incidents do sometimes occur, and when they do, can have a significant effect on staff morale in a school. The Committee recognised this and called for greater support for those teachers who had experienced violence (including support within the school; greater sensitivity to staff morale in the decisions of the Crown Prosecution Service; and the introduction of measures to compensate staff) (DES, 1989, pp. 191–4). Reaction in the press, however, indicated that many people failed to realise that the Elton Report, in indicating the exceptional nature of violent incidents, did not claim that all else was placid and perfect. Although the picture of a national crisis of discipline had been exaggerated, the Committee highlighted the urgent need for action to improve the current situation in many schools, especially with regard to frequent and wearing low level disruption. As a member of the Committee of Enquiry commented: 'We concluded that there is not a crisis in our schools but a cause for concern and a need for action' (Atkinson, 1989, p. ix).

The recommendations of the Elton Report indicated the variety of arenas in which schools might act, and there was considerable support (see Galloway et al, 1989; Hargreaves, 1989; Jones, 1989) for the idea that discipline should be thought about in terms of its relationship to academic learning and achievement and its relationship to whole-school organisational development. In planning the present study, therefore, we wanted to work with schools that were already thinking along these lines and were beginning to reconceptualise discipline as a unifying principle that affects pupil motivation, institutional purposefulness, and community understanding and support.

Exactly how a school sets about the task of reconceptualisation depends upon its level of self-knowledge, its values, and the strength of the traditions that hold habit in place. In short, each school, in trying to move forward, will be taking into account its past, its present and its possible futures. This complex process of development and accommodation is clearly seen in the five accounts that we offer of secondary schools in the process of rethinking discipline. The schools share a common concern for learning and, in particular, for the needs, aspirations and achievements of the individual learner.

The constellation of factors which makes each school distinctive means that the strategy and focus for development are likely to be different in each case. In one school the starting point is expectations; in another it is the building of a framework that supports consistency of practice; in one, dialogue is used to encourage participation and self-esteem; in another, the priority is to engage pupils actively in the task of learning; and in yet another the concern is with respect – self-respect and respect for others.

In this book, we refer to these focusing concepts – expectations, consistency, dialogue, engagement and respect – as *the dimensions of discipline*. They operate within and through a secure institutional framework of principles of procedure, sanctions and rewards, and they reflect widely held values and concerns. Importantly, they ensure that discipline is an educational matter not just a system of punishment and control.

The Schools and their Approaches

Our study was concerned with schools which, although situated in very different urban settings, were all experiencing levels of economic, environmental and social disadvantage that characteristically define 'inner- city' schools. We consulted census data in order to get an independent assessment of local conditions. Such data do not, of course, describe the population of particular schools, but they do offer a sketch of the economic and social context, at the level of the electoral ward, in which they are operating. The most recently available census data related to conditions in 1981, but there was no reason to believe that the areas had changed significantly over the last ten years.

In comparison with the electoral wards of all secondary schools in England and Wales, each of the five schools described in this book falls within the 25 per cent which have the highest rates of unemployment, the greatest proportion of children in households categorised as 'low' social class, and the greatest proportion of children from households which lack basic amenities (including, for example, inside toilets). In addition, three of the schools fall within the same band for further indicators of disadvantage, including the proportion of children in one-parent families and the proportion in large families (defined as households with four or more children). Such data tend to confirm the schools' view that they serve areas where relatively high proportions of pupils are likely to be disadvantaged. Thus, the contexts within which the new approaches to discipline are being developed offer a stern test and help to highlight issues which might remain hidden in less demanding settings.

In the chapters that follow, we try, using interview and documentary data, to present the ways in which the five schools are rethinking their approaches to discipline and some of the dilemmas they are experiencing. Some of the schools were only just embarking on the task of reconstruction while others were further along the way. For example, our account of Milner School (chapter 2), where a new head and deputy were working to raise expectations, highlights the slow and tentative processes whereby staff and pupils were coming to review their perceptions of one another. Central to this review was the school's determination to establish practice which is academically rigorous without losing the sense of caring which characterised its past.

In contrast, chapter 3 focuses on a school where the new approaches are relatively well established. Over a five-year period Reid

School has developed a systematic means of whole-school policy formation and implementation. The construction of a policy for discipline was an early priority. From a position of low morale, and poor relations between staff and senior management, the school has been able to build strong networks of peer support and to develop greater consistency in the way that teachers respond to pupils. Importantly, the staff have come to feel that they are part of a school where all teachers have a voice.

In Burran School (chapter 4) teachers are trying to build a collective commitment to dialogue as a means of helping pupils deal with incidents and behaviours that threaten progress and wellbeing. They are also using dialogue as a way of explaining the school's values and purposes to parents, as well as to pupils, so that there is a broader basis of understanding and support.

Progress in Seaview School (chapter 5) has been built upon a determination to increase the active engagement of pupils. Changes in assessment procedures in particular have helped to give pupils a greater sense of control over their own learning and behaviour.

The relationship between schools and their local communities is a complex one and raises some difficult issues. Tension and conflict can sometimes occur when there is a lack of understanding between school and community. Chapter 6 looks at the experiences of two schools which serve very different communities, Burran School – which also figures in chapter 4 – and Forest School. The accounts focus on attempts to improve respect for education as a potentially significant force in the lives of working-class people, and to heighten respect for learners in a school where the ethnic composition of the pupil population has changed markedly over a relatively short period.

The final chapter brings together some of the key issues emerging from the ways in which these schools have begun to rethink discipline.

Outline of the Research

Although we were limited in the amount of time we could spend in each school, we attempted to gather a range of data which would allow us to build a picture of each school's work from a variety of perspectives. Our data include interviews with teachers, pupils, parents and members of the local community; observations of meetings, classroom activities and interactions in corridors and around the school; documentary sources such as school guides, staff handbooks, attendance records and examination details. In each case, interview evidence forms the basis of our accounts.

In identifying urban schools that were seen to be making progress in relation to discipline we sought help from people who were likely to be well informed, including local inspectors and advisers, Her Majesty's Inspectors (HMI) and colleagues in higher education institutions. Our concern was to find schools that were making progress 'in a context of struggle and perseverance' – as we put it in our letters to schools – and where that progress was not a piecemeal affair but the result of a whole-school effort.

When a suitable school was identified we contacted the headteacher to outline the project and to gauge her or his interest in taking part. Subsequently one of us would visit the school to explain the study in more detail to the head and/or other staff, discuss current work in the school and gather preliminary documentary evidence. If, on reflection, both the school and the project team were keen to work together, a fieldwork timetable was drawn up. On some occasions unforeseen problems arose, often unconnected with the research, which meant that the pattern of contact with the school had to be modified. The expectation, however, was that fieldwork would involve a member of the project team spending several days in a school, either over time or *en bloc*.

In each school a similar range of interviews was requested, including pupils of various ages and teachers with different lengths of service and holding different positions of responsibility. The interview schedule was sometimes extended to gather more data on particular themes or to cover a greater variety of perspectives. In one school, for example, we conducted additional pupil interviews where we were particularly interested in the issue of pupil engagement with learning.

The chapters that follow report the ways in which schools are challenging taken-for-granted views of the nature of discipline and, in so doing, are developing new approaches and new interpretations of existing approaches. They reveal the complexity of the task but they also highlight the progress that can realistically be achieved.

2 Reconstructing Expectations

There is a tendency within schools to conceive of 'the discipline problem' in purely behavioural terms: as a recurring pattern of undesirable or unacceptable acts perpetrated by specific groups and individuals. Disciplinary systems have, accordingly, sometimes focused exclusively upon restraint and deterrence. The educational debate about discipline, in other words, has too often been a debate about indiscipline and about the kinds of institutional response that best curb and counter the effects of anti-social and disruptive behaviour within the school setting.

Two unfortunate consequences follow from this. First, less obvious forms of pupil disaffection and lack of motivation can be overlooked or seen as somehow different in kind from the more blatant manifestations of indiscipline. Thus, for example, pupils who are 'switched-off' or do just enough to 'get by' may not receive the support and encouragement that they require in order to progress and develop. Indeed, some teachers may, in order to avoid the risk of provoking more obvious acts of rejection or disruption, find themselves colluding with those pupils who, although not working to capacity, are at least not openly misbehaving. Such tacit arrangements (as Powell, Farrer and Cohen, 1985, illustrate) can have the effect over time of lowering the morale of teachers and pupils alike.

Second, discipline may well be seen, not as a positive achievement in itself, but as a kind of negative attribute: only the lack of it requires a response. This means that little attention is given to how discipline is acquired and how, once acquired, it may be sustained and developed within different situations. By this reckoning discipline is, at best, an externally-imposed rule system to which pupils adhere through habit, rather than a set of commitments that inform and focus pupils' attitudes to their work and to their working relationships.

This chapter explores a rather different approach, whereby 'the discipline problem' is defined, in part at least, in terms of the kinds of expectations that teachers have of their pupils and that pupils and teachers have of themselves. 'It is important', as Joan Lipsitz (1984, p. 187) reminds us, 'that teachers have high expectations for *themselves* and that they believe they are capable of making a difference in their pupils' learning.' From this perspective, discipline is – through and through – about reconstructing expectations. It is about creating a climate of trust and mutual respect in which pupil achievement and self-discipline are of prime importance.

Milner School: 'A Very Complex Dynamic'

This redefinition of 'the discipline problem' can usefully be related to the history and circumstances of a particular inner-city school. Milner School was the result of an amalgamation which took place in the early 1970s and which (in the words of one teacher who had lived through it) was 'horrendous':

> It was the amalgamation of four schools of different types. One was a boys' Technical High School as it used to be called; one was another secondary boys' school and the intake was extremely deprived; the other two schools were part of the same building, but it was like the Berlin Wall, the girls' secondary modern down one side and the boys' secondary modern down the other – and never the twain should meet, and didn't meet! There was quite a contrast because you had the boys coming in 'bovver boots' and denim jackets with insignia on the back and the girls in beautiful white knee-length socks and white blouses and blue skirts and tunics ... We had staff who didn't want to teach girls, staff who didn't want to teach boys, staff who didn't believe in comprehensive schools, staff who preferred the Grammar School type of pupil, etc, etc. So there was conflict between pupils, sometimes physical conflict between pupils, and – how can I put it politely? – idealistic conflict between members of staff.

Initially the amalgamated school operated across sites, which further exacerbated existing problems. As a head of year recalls:

> Two of the schools were almost a mile apart and, on occasion, I found myself teaching lesson six in this building, jumping in the car with a pile of books for lesson seven almost a mile up the road, passing

children being escorted from building to building ... It was a nightmare for discipline! To keep groups apart we used to let the Tech boys, for example, finish school fifteen minutes before the others so they could safely get away home at night.

The head who was appointed to oversee this amalgamation was, by all accounts, a woman of extraordinary strength and tenacity. According to another member of staff who had experienced the amalgamation, she saw it as her prime task to establish an effective pastoral system:

She had a strong background in pastoral work and I think she quite rightly saw that if she got people who had a good understanding of the role of pastoral staff it would help.

Recruitment was a crucial element in this strategy and part of the newly appointed head's distinctive style was that, as one teacher remembers, 'she made it quite clear that she wanted certain staff and didn't want others – in so many words!' Over time, therefore, the staff who survived knew that they enjoyed the support of the head and returned that support in the form of professional loyalty. Staff stability became a feature of the school, with a significant proportion of the staff having spent a large part of their professional lives in this one institution, some having first entered as probationers. This stability, moreover, was taken to be one of the head's greatest achievements and, throughout the 1970s and early to mid 1980s, was seen to be one of the main factors leading to the school's increasing success in dealing with pupils from a notoriously difficult inner-city area.

The vulnerability of a system built upon staff stability was highlighted when, in the mid 1980s, the school underwent further reorganisation leading to the redeployment of a significant number of teachers. One of those who had survived this period of reorganisation recalls its impact on the life of the school:

It was the quality of the staff who left actually. It was very difficult to replace them. We gained good staff but we also gained staff who really didn't want to come here; they were frightened of the school's reputation, they hadn't taught in a multicultural environment, and so on. They had reservations which actually showed through and children are very quick to pick up defensive attitudes ... It hit the head hard. She was in constant conflict with the LEA. The staff who stayed, we had to re-apply for our own jobs. I had to re-apply for my job and be interviewed by a General Adviser. Admittedly, it seemed more of a gesture than anything else, but nevertheless we didn't have job security at the time.

From this point on, that sense of Milner School being (as one teacher put it) 'our school, the teachers' school, the children's school, we are in it together, let's pull together' seems to have lost its magic. For a school that relied so much on cohesion and stability, this was a heavy blow. Besides, there were other changes on the horizon, which (however they were interpreted at the time) were, in retrospect, seen to render the old system still more vulnerable. As a long-standing member of the teaching staff now explains:

> I think the former head was realistic. I think perhaps she thought, 'Well I am of the old school' (and I don't mean the traditional school). I think perhaps she felt that she shouldn't be expected to introduce the ERA [Education Reform Act] and LMS [Local Management of Schools], and so on and so forth.

So, when a new head and deputy head were appointed, in the late 1980s, to a school that by now catered for around 850 pupils (with a sixth form numbering around sixty-five), a rather different kind of story began to emerge; a story, that is, which places the emphasis on managing change, rather than establishing stability. The newly appointed deputy notes:

> My impression of the school was of a fairly well-ordered community in which standards, as far as inter-personal relationships are concerned, were placed at a premium ... My second impression was that there was a need for change in a number of respects: the school had to be geared up to deal with GCSE [General Certificate of Secondary Education], the National Curriculum, and TVEI (Technical and Vocational Education Initiative).

What that need for change amounted to, as far as the new head-teacher was concerned, was a greater emphasis on pupil potential, teacher involvement and a facilitative style of school management. It was a need which had arisen, moreover, because of what he saw as a tacit trade-off between a kind of orderliness and the actual quality of pupil learning in the school:

> This school has been successful in the way in which it has approached the area of controlling youngsters and discipline and so on, because it does not put the demands upon youngsters that other schools may do. I have come in with a very clear view in my mind in terms of what I want to do as far as raising standards, if you like, in terms of academic achievement and ambition and self-esteem and vision for young people, and I have got to do that through the staff. The staff themselves have got to raise their aspirations for the young people and raise their vision and raise their expectations. There is a very complex dynamic there that may result in the institution itself going through some kind of radical turmoil that will upset the balance and equilibrium.

That same trade-off also operated at the managerial level, necessitating a parallel shift from what had previously been seen as 'strong management' to what the newly appointed deputy head characterised as 'a more participatory form of management whereby the onus ... for effective discipline, for decision-making and innovation, has moved down the system'. What is interesting about this school, then, is that we enter its history very much in the middle of things. Caught within its own 'very complex dynamic', its own peculiar (though generalisable) 'radical turmoil', it is trying to shift from being one kind of 'good' school to being a rather different kind of 'good' school:

> You have come to the school ... on the basis of an existing reputation for the way in which the school handled itself in a disciplinary sense and the kind of environment the school created for the students. You come on its previous reputation, whereas it is quite clear to many in the school that a major review and overhaul was needed.

The Dilemmas around Expectations

For some members of staff the changes being undertaken as part of this 'major review and overhaul' are associated with the imposition of a set of managerial and bureaucratic values that are juxtaposed against the caring values implicit in what they feel to be the best of the school's past. In such cases, the perceived shift of values is invariably seen as having a direct bearing on the school's disciplinary system, tilting it towards a more impersonal and less flexible approach to pupils. One teacher, for example, explains these changes in the following terms:

> They have a different style of management at the moment in the school. When I first came here, it was the most caring school I had ever been in . . . The style of management these days is more aloof, more distant, and there are rigid systems of punishment which have now to be adhered to. Whereas under the previous style of management there was give and there was take . . . For things like punishments, for example, we now have fairly set patterns of detentions. If they miss your own personal detention, they go on to a year head's detention; if they miss the year head's detention, they go on to a Faculty detention; if they come to you and say, 'But I've forgotten' or 'I lost my note', you can't say, 'Right, you will do it now'. They are automatically passed up the line.

Underlying this supposed dichotomy – between the 'caring school' and 'rigid systems of punishment', between a remembered past in which 'there was give and there was take' and an experienced present of 'set patterns of detention' – are certain assumptions about where pupils come from and what they need. In making explicit these assumptions and her attitude towards them, one of the teachers we interviewed seems to epitomise the positive, 'caring' aspects of the school's past:

> If you have got, as we have, children being continually put on detention for being late and if you ferret in there and you find out a bit more, you realise that mummy is a prostitute and daddy is in prison. They [our pupils] have got to get the children ready for school, as well as themselves, and take them there. We are expecting too much of them.

But are we? This is the crucial issue which, from a different perspective, may have less to do with where pupils come from than with where they see themselves going and how the school can help them get there. The distinction is a difficult one, since origins undoubtedly influence destinations. Nevertheless, schools, while not compensating for society, might perhaps be part of a more general, more diversified, reconstruction of society. That, at least, is how the following teacher sees it:

> There is no reason why, because the kids live in this area and come to this school, we should accept lower standards in any field or in any area. Because the kids come from a deprived area, from an area of high unemployment or from an area where there is high crime and poor housing stock, it does not mean to say that they have got to come into an institution like this and put up with a second-rate version of themselves.

Another teacher agrees. She too makes certain assumptions about the background of her pupils, but this time those assumptions are related quite explicitly to her own background as a member of an ethnic minority community. In trying to make sense of how, as a head of year, she should begin to exercise responsibility for the pastoral oversight of her pupils, expectations are again the central issue. But this time that issue is neither about accepting received expectations, nor about raising them. It is about reinterpreting them from within:

> What my father taught us was that you don't criticise, you keep your head down, you get where you want to be, you make sure you are inside the system and once you are inside the system somebody has got to listen to you and that is when you can change it. He used to say: 'You are in front of a brick wall. You can't knock that brick wall down because it is too solid. You can't climb over that wall, because there is glass on the top and there are dogs waiting to be set upon you. The only way you can get through that door is to become "well educated". Once you are "well educated" they will allow you through that door. Leave it a couple of years until you are well established, when people realise that you are a normal human being (and that if they cut you, you will bleed). And then you start to change it, and then you start to organise it. Don't be loud about it, don't be boisterous about it,

because people will then just turn their back on you. You do it subtly, you do it quietly and you try and make it look as though they are the ones who are doing the changing and not you. Let them think that they thought about it first.' I think that is really what I am trying to get over ... if you start shouting, if you start trying to knock down the wall, people are more likely to make another wall – to ensure that you don't get in.

One way of reading this is as an attempt, by the teacher, to resolve the problem of how, in good faith, she might act *in loco parentis*; how her identification with the history and culture of the child might inform the pupil–teacher relationship in such a way as to extend the child's horizons. Her particular response may have its limitations, but the problem to which it points is fundamental. It is a problem, moreover, that is located both in the history of the school and in her own personal biography: What does it mean to care for someone in such a way that one wants the very best for them? When does care shade off into indulgence? When is it sharpened to the point of severity?

Not everyone in the Milner School agrees on the answer to these questions, but there is widespread agreement that they are the right questions to ask. There is also a growing awareness of the extent to which any adequate response to these questions is likely to represent a serious challenge to the professional identity of many teachers. For any such response must acknowledge not only that teachers are important role models but that the particular models they present may require considerable redefinition.

Some important gender issues are at stake here and these have a direct bearing on the quality of pupil–teacher relationships within the school. Several interviewees mentioned, for example, that male teachers may face a particular problem in that many of the boys' experience of men is such that they expect their male teachers to be 'hard' and 'macho' and some of the girls' experience is such that they see them as a sexual threat. The attempt to establish relationships that are unequivocally acknowledged, by pupils and teachers alike, to be based on a caring regard for educational achievement may, in other words, involve a

16

review of the versions of masculinity and femininity prevailing within the school and of how these relate to notions of teacher professionalism.

In attempting to resolve the dilemmas it has inherited from the past, Milner School relies heavily upon the independent judgements of its teachers and their willingness to think critically about their own practice. This requires great versatility and variety of approach. In spite of a few teachers' sense of the increased rigidity of the new management system, there is no suggestion that every teacher should know in advance exactly how he or she would react in a particular situation, nor that every teacher should necessarily react in exactly the same way within that situation. What is new is the expectation that teachers should themselves be centrally concerned with translating agreed values into a coherent and consistent set of practices and that their active involvement in this process is what renders them fully professional.

Emphasis on Learning

Central to these agreed values is a renewed emphasis on pupils' and teachers' commitment to learning and on school discipline as an expression of that commitment. In a sense, of course, this is true of any school that aspires to be effective. Milner School, however, has added a useful gloss to what might otherwise be a truism. In the practical working out of its emphasis on learning, the school places a high premium on the need to:

- acknowledge the range and variety of learning that takes place within the school;

- offer firm and directive pastoral support through the day-to-day interactions between pupils and teachers and through the tutorial system; and

- plan carefully at both the classroom and whole-school levels for high academic achievement and for personal and social understanding.

What is perhaps most remarkable about these themes is that they exist side by side. Schools that acknowledge a variety of pupil achievements are not uncommon; nor schools that have a distinctly interventionist line on tutorial support; nor schools that plan for high academic achievement and that take seriously the personal and social education of their pupils. But a school that puts these together is likely to confound some of the timeworn distinctions (between, for example, 'academic' and 'vocational', 'progressive' and 'traditional', 'disciplined' and 'caring') and, in so doing, to challenge our preconceptions as to what constitutes a 'good' school. It is how the themes relate – how they begin to add up to a culture and a climate – that is of importance.

A crucial factor in ensuring that they do relate is the school's insistence on the equal valuing of people and the importance of developing all aspects of the person. The reward system that has been instituted is an important expression of these values: pupils, for example, receive credit for good attendance, for sustained effort in the classroom, for carefully completed homework assignments and for the general standard of their behaviour in and around the school. Achievements in these areas are acknowledged and celebrated in school assemblies and in reports to parents. This is much more than a carrot-on-the-end-of-a-stick approach. It is, as the headteacher maintains, an attempt to acknowledge the diversity of achievement within the school and to ground that acknowledgement in an ethics of respect for the whole person:

> We are not just concentrating on the cognitive aspects of personal development here, although traditionally that is what schools are about. We are looking at the development of the whole child. I actually believe that is very, very important. That is a fundamental value.

Where the emphasis on learning is most pronounced, however, and where its impact is felt most strongly by the pupils, is in their daily interactions with their teachers and in the regular contact with their pastoral tutors. It is at this point that the traditional dichotomy between 'pastoral' and 'academic' breaks down irreparably. For it is generally acknowledged among the staff that, as David Galloway (1990, pp. 64–5) puts it, 'effective teaching requires a "moral climate" in the classroom which facilitates communication within the class on matters relevant to the children's welfare outside it'. What we learn from this school is that,

DIMENSIONS OF DISCIPLINE

where the quality of pupil learning is a priority, a high premium must be placed on the quality of the relationships between teachers and pupils:

> If the nature of the relationship between the teacher and the pupils is right, everything else fits into place. You can almost always trace ill-discipline to that one single factor: the nature and quality of the relationships and the actual learning process itself.

Instituting a reward system, although an important aspect of the school's disciplinary system, is not, therefore, in itself enough. Any attempt to create a school climate that is characterised by high pupil expectations and a strong sense of professional purpose requires a great deal more than the setting up and maintenance of such a system. It is, as one of the senior teachers within the school maintains, the pupil–teacher relationships, and the interactions they give rise to, that provide the context within which rewards gain significance and without which they are reduced to a mere bureaucratic exercise:

> More than anything, the words are important – and the relationships. All the other things in a sense come later. I wouldn't like to see a school where there were all kinds of tangible reward systems, and yet the intangible – the personal – are missing.

One point that emerges strongly from the interviews in this school is that the pupils have a very clear sense of the teachers whom they feel are 'on their side'. Such teachers, according to the pupils, tend to share certain characteristics. They are, as in the following (Year 10) pupil's description of her teacher, calm and understanding, but they also set limits and make demands. Indeed, the demand by her teacher that she 'do something about it' is, for this particular pupil, one of the reasons why that teacher is 'just one of the best':

> He listens to everything. Like if you have got any views about things, he will listen to them. If you do something wrong, he like drums it into us that we are not supposed to do it. He doesn't scream like, you know, across the classroom like many of the teachers do. He just talks to us and says, 'Come on now, buckle down, do something about it'.

In the four years I've been here I think our teacher is just one of the best. He never shouts. He always talks calmly and, like, sorts it out.

Another teacher explains how, for her, this kind of calm, supportive relationship, that nevertheless makes serious demands on pupils, underlies her own work as a pastoral tutor:

I always, without fail, make them tell me what they want me to do and, to the best of my ability, I attempt to do just that. I also try to give them a chance to come back to me and say, 'Well, I wasn't satisfied with the way in which you dealt with it'. For my part, it puts the onus on them, because I am not acting off my own back: they told me what they want me to do and I will try and do it. If it goes wrong, 'Well, I only did what you asked me to do'. Even if it is something silly like not having a pen, 'Well, what would you like me to do?' 'Well, you can lend me one?' 'All right.' That sort of thing.

What comes across again and again from the interview evidence is, as David Hargreaves (1972, p. 263) once put it, that 'caring for and trust in the child are not skills as such, but rather assumptions, attitudes or approaches taken by the teacher towards the pupil'. So, for the head-teacher, the fundamental issue about 'being on their side' is a value issue:

The issue about being on their side is related to – 'It is not you that I disapprove of, it is your actions and your behaviour that I disapprove of, but not you as a person.' This is a very important distinction because for many young people it can often seem to be the 'you', as opposed to the 'behaviour', that is being criticised. So that is related very clearly to a set of personal values that individuals have themselves or a set of corporate values that exists within the school ... First and foremost among these fundamental values – the non-negotiables if you like – are the equal valuing of people and the importance of developing all aspects of a person.

The school places great emphasis on ensuring that these 'non-negotiables' work their way through into the minutiae of curriculum planning. To this end, it has (as the curriculum deputy puts it) 'moved more towards curriculum-led management', with the role of faculty heads having been more clearly defined in terms of 'curriculum leadership':

> If there is effective planning, if there are clearly recognisable short-term goals for pupils, and if there is teaching consistency at the outset, then you are setting the groundwork really for effective discipline without in fact using disciplinary measures. It is the climate that you need to create ... In that sense, discipline is part and parcel of the planning of activities. It isn't something which arises independently of activities.

The school has also recently undertaken an extensive curriculum review. This involved an audit, through curriculum areas, of existing school policy and practice with regard to teaching and learning methods, together with a pupil monitoring exercise that focused on a cross-section of Year 10 pupils and on the Year 8 pupil reports. As a result of this review, the school has identified some areas of concern to which all teachers are now paying particular attention. These include: pupils' personal organisation and preparedness for lessons (in relation, for example, to equipment); attendance and punctuality throughout the school day; and pupils' attitudes to, and completion of, homework assignments.

The role of the pastoral tutor is acknowledged to be of vital importance in all these areas, but particularly with regard to the monitoring of homework. An internal school document highlights a set of specific needs within this area to which house and year staff are currently responding:

- we need a homework timetable and information about coursework – available to parents and posted in all tutor bases;

- tutors need to check that homework is being set and that it is being done;

- we need a standard means of communicating information from subject teachers to tutors;

- we need a standard means of information about homework and progress to parents; and

- tutors need to support each other in these arrangements.

Attention to detailed planning relates also to the pastoral curriculum. An important change in this area is the formation of a team of seven teachers who are responsible for designing and teaching a personal and social development course for all pupils. The team liaises closely with form tutors, who previously carried out whatever social and personal education took place within their own form periods, and are resourced in part by the subject departments. The shift towards a smaller team of teachers, which comprises three women and four men (two of whom are members of the senior management team), is intended to facilitate curriculum planning and achieve a more coherent pastoral programme across the whole school.

It is as yet early days, but so far the response from parents and pupils to this particular curriculum innovation has been positive. One member of the team suggests, for example, that the course was already helping pupils to interact more favourably with one another and to settle their differences more amicably:

> The tutor said that they worked as a group much better. They became a bit more interactive and friendly towards each other. One of the pupils had been badly name-called – 'slag', 'slut', that sort of thing – and they were able to sort it out for themselves. Because that was one of the issues that came up on the course.

What we can take from this single case by way of a lesson – an exemplar – is that the real challenge for secondary schools is not only to their teaching and managerial skills, or their organisational structures, but also to their educational values: 'it is the climate that you need to create'. This is not to say that teaching skills and organisational structures are unimportant, but that what importance they have can only be realised by schools that are willing to replace some of the old dichotomies with a renewed emphasis on a more rounded and holistic approach to learning. Education, insofar as it is value-driven, must be concerned with the growth and development of the whole person.

The Story Continued: Some Unresolved Issues

But this, we must remember, is a school in transition. There is, as its teachers know and readily acknowledge, a number of issues which remain unresolved. What they do not as yet know is whether these issues can in fact be resolved (and if so how and by whom) or whether their lack of resolution is just another inner-city problem that has to be lived with. Either way they present themselves as difficult choices between important, but potentially competing, sets of priorities.

One of these issues concerns the kinds of tension that may be engendered within a school that is committed to raising the expectations of both staff and pupils. A number of teachers feel that the demands that are now being put upon them, and that they themselves are putting upon their pupils, may give rise to a range of other problems:

> If, for example, I am picking up in the last four or five weeks a dozen or so fights, then is that because the weather is windy and wet? Or is it because we are now expected to have higher expectations and that, because the youngsters themselves are not always able to meet those expectations, they are maybe frustrated and anxious?

This frustration and anxiety could also have implications regarding patterns of attendance and punctuality within the school. While there is no evidence of a sharp increase in absences, the general level of absenteeism remains a cause of concern. So the school has to ask itself whether the relation between expectations and achievement might not be more complex than at first appears and, indeed, whether (in the short term at least) the increased demands made on pupils and teachers might not manifest themselves in disturbing, or even disruptive, patterns of behaviour and attendance.

A second unresolved issue relates to teaching styles and implicit notions of orderliness. Among the teaching staff there is general agreement on the need to develop a more interesting and relevant curriculum and to highlight the importance of active and participatory classroom experiences. Indeed, this emphasis on increasing the involvement of pupils, raising their motivation, and engendering a strong commitment to work and achievement, is central to the school's attempt at reconstruction.

At the same time, however, there is some concern among the teaching staff that, by encouraging pupils to take responsibility for their own learning, they are creating situations in which pupils can, and do, choose to behave irresponsibly. This point is made strongly by one of the heads of faculty:

> Whereas you may get a majority of kids who understand the task and what they have to do and any objectives you have given them for the lesson, there are always going to be some who will seek to use the opportunity for some other end. I have just been teaching a first year class who, on the whole, I consider to be a very good class, a very co-operative class, but there are, say, four individuals in the class whose behaviour makes them stand out. They are active in their indiscipline. They are actively seeking opportunities primarily to amuse themselves and, I suspect also, to rope others in.

Part of the problem here is that the school's more recent emphasis on pupil participation and involvement allows teachers to see evasions and refusals that, within a more traditional system, tended to remain hidden. When pupils were expected to do only what they were told, they could get by without any real commitment to the learning tasks. Now that they are expected to think for themselves, any lack of commitment is both visible and problematic. So, while nobody in the school wants to go back, moving forward is acknowledged to be extremely difficult.

A third issue relates to the time constraints operating on teachers. In other settings this emphasis on the lack of time might be seen as a defensive reaction against change. However, these particular teachers have shown themselves quite willing to respond to the changing climate and to adapt their practices accordingly. Their worries about the amount of time spent on what they call 'paperwork' cannot, therefore, be lightly dismissed:

> It is a common complaint among teachers, isn't it, that you have so little time? You are under such pressure to fulfil certain tasks that you find yourself just running around after the paperwork. You just don't have the time to sit down and talk out their problems with the chil-

dren you teach. You fill in one form, then on to the next lesson, fill in the next set of forms and, in between, somewhere along the way, try and fit in the children. There is just not the time. And these children need time more than anything else. They and their parents need time.

These are teachers, it should be emphasised, who realise the importance of 'paperwork' as a means of recording their pupils' attainment and of plotting their progress on a regular basis, and who would see that cumulative record as informing the kind of talk that they want to engage in with their pupils. They are not against 'paperwork' as such, but they do see a clash of priorities between the routine monitoring and administrative functions they are expected to perform and the day-to-day contact that they need, and want, to maintain with their pupils. If they are against anything, it is what they see as the increasing bureaucratisation of their role as teachers.

A fourth and final issue focuses on the need to translate raised expectations into positive achievements and on the inherent risks of failing to do so. 'You've got to change your basic approach', as one teacher puts it; and, in so doing, you have got to make a serious impact on the quality of learning in the classroom:

> If you don't, the more you raise your expectations the worse the situation is going to get – because the more frustrated you're going to feel. It's not just that expectations need raising. It's that our pupils need to see that they can achieve. There's some sort of subtle difference there I think.

Currently, Milner School is very much concerned with that 'subtle difference'. Having appreciated how important expectations are, its staff are now trying to ensure that these are fully reflected in the range and quality of pupil achievements within the school. This, of course, is a long-term project and one that will necessarily take time. It is not just that an old kind of orderliness based on compliance and constraint is being questioned, but that the new order of negotiation and consensus is extraordinarily difficult to achieve. For a school that is trying to turn itself around, as this one is, progress may in the short-term be patchy and by no means all of a piece. Any advance must be a matter of small, deliberate steps forward on several fronts at once.

Conclusions

Discipline cannot be divorced from other aspects of schooling. It is part of a school's whole way of life and, as such, is implicit in its overall aims and practices. In this particular chapter we have tried to relate discipline to the notion of expectations. Pupil achievement, we have argued, is dependent upon the expectations that pupils have of themselves and that their teachers have for them. Problems which manifest themselves as essentially disciplinary can very often, therefore, be traced back to a downward spiral of low expectations and chronic underachievement. By this reckoning, a disciplined school is a school not only with a sense of purpose, but with a sense of purpose that is communicated to, and internalised by, the pupils themselves; a school that is intent upon becoming 'a knowable community' (see Nixon, 1992).

The school that we have discussed above is still learning and developing. It is placing a high premium on the recognition of a wide range of pupil achievement, the strengthening of tutorial support, and increased attention to coherent curriculum planning. It is also learning that whole-school change takes time; that any improvement in one area of school life is likely to throw up unforeseen problems in other areas; and that teachers are more likely to respond to those problems with speed and sensitivity in a non-hierarchical system in which bureaucracy is kept to a minimum.

Any final judgement regarding the school's success in responding to its own redefinition of 'the discipline problem' would be premature. Milner School can, however, fairly claim that it has begun to set the standards by which it can eventually be judged and by which it can judge itself. Unresolved issues remain, but at least the school is clear about the kind of problem it is tackling and the kind of response it is developing. It has, in other words, taken a hard look at the notion of school discipline and is relating this to the attitudes and aspirations that teachers have for themselves and one another, for their pupils, and for the quality of learning in their classrooms.

26

3 Working for Consistency

A good deal of work on discipline in schools stresses the importance of consistency in the way teachers identify and respond to disorder. For example, in their report *Good Behaviour and Discipline in Schools*, HMI outline several areas of 'good practice'. Among nine items on 'leadership' are these:

> Creating the conditions for *agreement about the standards* to be expected and about how they will be achieved;
>
> seeing to it that such standards are *consistently applied*;
>
> *(HMI, 1989, para. 14: emphasis added)*

Whilst the document calls for schools' aims and policies to be 'applied consistently and fairly' (para. 13), it also states the need for flexibility 'to suit individual circumstances' (para. 43). The problem of being simultaneously 'consistent' and 'flexible' is a difficult one to resolve. It is neither possible, nor desirable, that schools dictate to staff a list of set responses for each occasion where pupils' behaviour fails to meet expectations. And yet the problem of matching consistency and flexibility is crucial: research on pupil perspectives has shown how keenly they judge teachers' 'fairness' in dealings with different pupils (Woods, 1983). One way forward is to establish a set of clearly articulated principles which all staff recognise and seek to put into practice. This is a difficult task which has important consequences for policy and decision-making within schools, and for the ways in which staff seek to support colleagues in their dealings with disciplinary issues.

This chapter examines the ways in which a school staff have begun to articulate the key values which drive their work and which help them to act in ways which are generally consistent. This is not, of course, to say that complete uniformity of outlook can – or will ever – be achieved. The goal is rather to achieve a high degree of professional commitment to a set of key values which all staff recognise and try to put into action. The analysis highlights the vital role of school management approaches which seek to inform and actively involve all staff in policy formation.

Reid Community School

Reid is an 11–16 community school which serves an area of severe economic disadvantage. The vast majority of pupils are drawn from the Marshall estate, a large area of council housing which is traditionally thought to have been used as the local authority's post-War dumping ground for 'problem families'. The Marshall estate has a history and a culture which maintain its isolation from the rest of the city. It is difficult for outsiders to appreciate the strength of the barriers until they seek to cross them. A member of the senior management team notes:

> Marshall has a particular culture/sub-culture where certain standards reign that don't pertain in many of the staff's local communities and you learn by experience as to what your involvement is on the estate and what it ought not to be ... One of our very strong Heads of Year happened to be driving through the estate (about 10 years ago) and he broke up a fight – there were about 50, 70 people there. The next day one of the bigger lads came into the fifth year and said, 'Mr X, you shouldn't have done that last night, had it not been *you*, you would have been hospitalised ... You should have let that fight sort itself out, you can't interfere in our estate. Stay out mate.'

Most children rarely venture beyond the confines of the estate. Large family networks extend throughout the community, and these can act as a source of both cohesion and conflict. Although the school's traditional catchment area extends beyond the estate and into Wood Way – an affluent middle-class area – very few pupils are drawn from outside Marshall. The estate has a city-wide reputation and those Wood Way parents who do not use the private sector mostly choose to send their children to alternative state schools. A teacher in her second year at Reid recalls others' reactions to the news that she was to work there:

> As soon as I said I was teaching in Marshall everyone was up in arms, they couldn't believe that anyone would *dare* teach in Marshall ... It

wasn't just teachers, it was all sorts of people – *relatives* – anybody, when I said I was going to teach in Marshall they were really quite frightened for me.

Reputations such as this can be wildly exaggerated. One of two full-time Educational Welfare Officers (EWOs) attached to the school recognises the danger of stereotyping the community, but also acknowledges the very real problems which some pupils face:

> There are some very nice people out there, some very, *very* adequate parents, but there are a lot that aren't. A lot of the children haven't got the facility to study at home or there is no communication between parents. [Children] will go home, they will get themselves something to eat quickly and they will go out. And then they will come in to go to bed. Or the opposite of that, they will come in, they will have to clean the house, they will have to look after siblings ...

One of the school's most experienced teachers (more than twenty years spent at Reid) confesses that 'we are all quite frequently shocked by some of the things that we hear that have happened in the kids' backgrounds'. In fact, the teachers' shared understanding of the conditions under which some of their pupils live was a key factor in the development of a cohesive set of principles which now guide the school. A recognition of the importance of individual needs is especially strong in Reid: it is expressed through strategies which seek to avoid confrontation and build upon positive experiences and relationships:

> Caring is important and I think people discover quite early on that in the majority of cases if you are experiencing a discipline problem . . . the traditional 'heavy hand' is not always the most successful way of dealing with it. It is much better to have a more cajoling attitude and again, I suppose, trying to make the kids see that what you are actually doing is caring for them: you are not trying to make them do something because it makes you feel better but because it is actually better for them.
>
> *(A teacher of more than twenty years' experience in the school)*

It is significant that many long-serving teachers feel that, because of the particular problems and demands which the community presents, something of this caring and positive attitude has always been present in the school. However, the confident whole-school approaches to teaching and future development which are now evident have only been achieved within the last five years. When we probed the reasons for the school's current strength, the single factor which teachers most often drew to our attention concerned the participative management style which a new headteacher had established.

When the new head was appointed, in the mid 1980s, there was a strong sense of disarray and morale was extremely low. The school was emerging from a very difficult period which had included an ambitious building programme, curriculum restructuring and, of course, two years of prolonged industrial conflict which had led to the withdrawal of teachers' 'goodwill'. When he arrived, therefore, the new head inherited a school which was fragmented: there was a widespread feeling that the school lacked a sense of direction. A teacher of considerable experience at Reid remembers that the period had left many teachers feeling disheartened and unimportant:

> Where [the new head] has done a good job is that he has actually brought back people's own self respect. Because at one stage the morale of this staff was rock bottom ... Back in '85, I have never seen such a demoralised school in my life ...

One of the headteacher's first priorities was to assess and regulate the stress under which teachers were operating. Like their colleagues in many schools, for example, Reid staff felt that the schedule of after-school meetings had become unworkable. In addition to daily briefings before school, most staff were involved in after-school meetings, sometimes accounting for four evenings out of five. The head put a freeze on the proliferating meeting pattern and canvassed opinion about possible solutions. In order to obviate the need for after-school meetings a system was initiated whereby (one day a week) staff arrive early and school starts thirty-five minutes later than usual. This creates a block of around fifty minutes which is used for whole-staff meetings and in-service education and training (INSET). In addition, each subject area has a timetable allocation such that at some point each week the whole department have a free lesson in which to hold subject meetings.

The arrangements did not, of course, put an end to all after-school meetings but they did identify a regular time slot when the whole staff could come together to work on issues that were important for them. The atmosphere at these meetings is different: teachers arrive ready to work rather than tired at the end of the school day. Crucially, the change signalled that teachers' fatigue was taken seriously. The new meeting has now become a basic part of the machinery through which the whole staff identify problems and seek workable and consistent solutions. Before considering this further, however, it is necessary to understand the importance of the Reid Values Statement. The significance of this document lies not only in its role as a statement of institutional priorities, but also as a model for the kinds of process through which whole-school developments can be managed within the school.

Making Values Explicit

We had to give the place some sense of direction and purpose and I think that was where the creation of our values structure came into place. We stumbled on that almost by accident but it has turned out probably to be the most important thing that we have ever done because that gave the real *keystones* of what we were about.

(Headteacher)

Although the head came to a school with low teacher morale, many staff shared a common sense of 'what we are about'. Several teachers had been attracted to Reid by the very features which frightened most-middle class parents away: teaching children from the estate is an extremely challenging job, but it is one that many find rewarding and believe they are good at. Trying to build upon some of these positive features, the head began a process which aimed to recognise the points of success which are often overlooked in inner-city locations: 'We got into the business of trying to say, "What is Reid good at?", rather than "What is Reid bad at?".'

The attempt to identify the school's strengths began as a very modest exercise but it crucially avoided the trap, of which many newly appointed headteachers fall foul, of seeming to disregard previous work in the institution (Weindling and Earley, 1987). Furthermore, the process touched on the deeply held commitments of the staff and revealed a unity of purpose which had previously not been recognised, let alone articulated.

The process began with a trawl through various school documents, brochures and press cuttings. Unfortunately, nothing emerged which satisfied the staff's belief that there was 'something unique' about the school. Finally a group of about fifteen people (including teaching, support and ancillary staff) tried to 'brainstorm' ideas which reflected their view on the questions 'what do we stand for? and what do we stand against?' Eventually, the head produced a first draft which was considered and modified by a series of meetings, culminating in whole-staff discussions as part of a statutory training day.

The document which emerged, the Reid Values Statement, made explicit (for the first time) the shared thinking which staff believed should drive their work. The document consists of a series of statements, including: 'we care for all our members, past and present'; 'each member is encouraged to make the most of their ability and to achieve a sense of personal worth'; 'we recognise that we are a part of a wider community – we must take care to work closely with people and organisations around us'; 'we must be proud of our successes and capable of recognising and learning from our failures'. The document ends with the statement, *'Above all, each member must, each day, achieve a little bit of success'.*

The values statement took a long time to create, partly because priority was given to more routine and immediately pressing concerns. As the head notes:

> It took two years to get it written down. Although it was there all the time, it was implicit ... We were going at it a little bit at a time and feeling our way, but I think it was far better than going in on a 'Here's a flip-chart; let's think up ten aims for a school'. I think the methodology was highly appropriate.

DIMENSIONS OF DISCIPLINE

The statement which emerged was more than a mere summary of past feelings and priorities. Although the exercise started as a somewhat *ad hoc* way of identifying strengths and seeking a sense of direction, the statement (and the process by which it was created) came to represent a standard against which staff believed current and future activities should be measured:

> I don't think we realised the power of what we were dealing with until we had done it and *then* we realised that we had actually got our hands on something that could be used as a springboard for everything else we do in the school.

Although the values statement had taken a long time to create, the process had successfully drawn upon – and made explicit – basic commitments which were widely shared among staff. Additionally, the means by which the statement had been created presented the school with the beginnings of a model for ways in which the whole staff could be involved in addressing a range of pressing issues (which they would identify) and which demanded whole-school responses.

Whole-School Policy Formation

The headteacher at Reid does not claim to be democratic on all occasions. He argues that a person's managerial 'style' should reflect the demands of particular situations and problems: 'You have to match the style to the issue. And so staff have got to be schooled in that process and comfortable with it; that one will be democratic on some occasions and autocratic on others.' Handled badly such a managerial philosophy could be interpreted as indecisive and unpredictable – leadership traits which are not generally welcomed by teachers (Becker, 1953; Weindling and Earley, 1987; Gillborn, 1991). The fact that Reid's teachers seem at ease with this style reflects not only the head's good judgement over when to be autocratic, but also the genuine sense of 'ownership' which staff feel over many key areas:

> On some issues he won't consult; some issues you just *have* to make a decision there and then – which is fair enough. And I think people accept that, *providing* you select the right issues for consultation ...

'Issue groups' are being set up to discuss various important issues – such as behaviour – so *all* staff are involved in that, from senior to the newest member of staff. And it is a *genuine* consultation.

The system of consultation based on 'issue groups' (mentioned above) makes use of the meeting slot created by the delayed start to one school day each week. The system provides a forum where a range of staff can consider, in some detail and over a period of time, a particular problem which is thought to require whole-school action. A series of 'issue groups' operate each year. Initially the new headteacher selected the issues to be addressed but that function has now been assumed by the whole staff: 'multicultural policy', 'role of INSET' and 'library development' are among the groups working at present.

Once a series of issues has been identified (using statutory INSET time) each member of staff signs up for a group. The 'issue groups' meet regularly and, during each half-term, report back to the whole staff who consider progress and offer critical comments and advice on future areas of concern which the group should address. Throughout their deliberations the 'issue groups' are expected to consider how their progress matches up to the values statement. Any anomalies or areas of ambiguity are presented to the whole staff. A cycle of discussion (within the 'issue group') and regular reporting back (to the whole staff) is intended, by the end of the third term, to lead to the formation of a whole-school policy which is understood by all staff.

The system of consultation has recently been extended to include 'maintenance groups'. These take over from 'issue groups' once a policy is in place, monitoring and evaluating the translation of policy into practice. The development is interpreted by teachers as a further sign of the head's preparedness to work *with* the staff at a pace which they can handle. As a head of year notes:

> He lets it go at the pace which he thinks is acceptable. And he is prepared to have his ideas halted, slowed down or just marking time. And then the pace picks up again when he feels it is about right ...

Our interviews with teachers produced a good deal of evidence that the system was particularly successful in generating a shared sense of participation and ownership. The teachers feel that their voices are heard: they understand, and have the opportunity to influence, the direction of future developments. The consultation system is, therefore, a practical attempt to involve the whole staff in the process of identifying the pressing concerns for the school, and then addressing what should be done about them bearing in mind the school's agreed values. The main aim of the process is to produce positive, realistic policies which help move the school forward. It is interesting that 'discipline' was one of the very first issues which staff wanted to address. The way in which a discipline policy has been produced and applied offers a further insight into the ways in which coherent and consistent approaches have been built, sustained and – perhaps most importantly – communicated to pupils.

A Policy on Behaviour

The decision to address discipline through one of the very first 'issue groups' reflected a general concern among staff that they needed to clarify their thinking and practice in that area. A member of the senior team feels that the behaviour policy was prompted by a 'groundswell' of staff opinion which focused on the issue of consistency in staff expectations and responses to pupil behaviour. The 'issue group' produced a behaviour policy which has now been adopted by the whole staff. The policy begins by emphasizing the importance of coherence and consistency as related to the school values statement:

> The values statement sets out the way we should react to one another within the organisation. It has as its corner-stones the concepts of caring and success ... A behaviour policy must build from these concepts and must provide practical action for ensuring that we live up to our values.

Building from this, the policy goes on to present clear and simple guidance on the responsibilities of both staff and pupils. Pupils, for example, are required to be 'polite', 'punctual', 'well presented', 'honest' and 'trustworthy'. The policy statement also emphasises that 'verbal and physical abuse/violence is unacceptable' and that 'our high expectations of pupils must be matched by high expectations of ourselves'. Specific advice to teachers includes 'respecting our values system and interpreting the needs of the pupils sensitively', and concludes by stating, 'avoid confrontation and seek help. Be flexible but define the boundaries'.

In line with good practice reported elsewhere, the behaviour policy attempts to 'establish clear and defensible principles and set the boundaries of acceptable behaviour' (HMI, 1989, p. 28). In addition to the details set out above, however, the document also includes a short additional 'check list' of 'some dos and don'ts' such as 'don't wear coats in class'. During its first year of operation, some teachers interpreted the policy as a list of rules rather than a set of principles. Consequently, they tried rigidly to enforce statements such as 'no coats in the classroom'. As a result, many lessons started with teacher–pupil conflict. In turn the teachers complained that some of their colleagues were not enforcing the rule and thereby failing to be consistent. When we visited the school the 'maintenance group' was still considering such problems: there was evidence, however, that people were recognising that the list of 'dos and don'ts' was not in keeping with the school values statement and the principles outlined elsewhere in the behaviour policy. As a member of the 'maintenance group' told us:

> There are some staff, particularly the newer staff, who have read the behaviour policy and are insisting on almost interpreting it by the letter, whereas the older hands are letting things go ... because staff may recognise that it is more important to have a positive learning atmosphere in the room rather than have a battle for the first 10 minutes.

In addition to specific concerns such as this, the 'maintenance group' also found itself dealing with more fundamental issues such as inequalities of power within the staff body. Like many other schools the majority of promoted staff in Reid are male. Although the system of 'issue groups' and 'maintenance groups' is still establishing itself in the school, there are indications that the system is empowering staff to raise difficult problems which have previously gone unrecognised and/or unspoken. One of the most important problems which the discipline 'maintenance group' has raised, for example, concerns the gendered messages about power and authority which are implicitly transmitted where promoted male staff intervene in female teachers' lessons.

It is clear, therefore, that when we visited Reid the staff were still in the process of identifying and working through existing inconsistencies and other areas of concern. Yet the very fact that these issues had such a high profile in staff discussions is a measure of the success of the consultation system and the staff's willingness to share their concerns. Furthermore, there are indications that the process has already heightened people's awareness of certain issues and, in some cases, had a real impact in classrooms. A teacher told us, for example:

> I have become a lot more aware of areas to concentrate on and I find myself thinking that I must keep my eye on whatever things may have been slack in the past. So it has certainly raised my awareness.

Whole-school policies in Reid (such as the one which focuses on behaviour and disciplinary issues) are, therefore, the result of a formal structure which is designed to involve all staff in the identification and resolution of pressing concerns. This structure helps to sustain a cohesive, supportive climate, and enables staff to respond sensitively and consistently to disciplinary issues.

The design and application of formal policies, however, is only part of the story. In order fully to understand the institution it is necessary to examine the day-to-day processes which support and extend the positive approaches (emphasising caring and achievement) which are explicitly recognised in school policy. The various means of peer support, within the staff body, both complement and extend the shared professional commitment to values which is developing through the processes of policy formation and implementation.

Peer Support

Ability as a classroom manager is often seen as a prerequisite for good teaching. To seek advice from colleagues can sometimes feel like an admission of failure, especially if the response is an example of what a teacher once described to us as 'the he's-all-right-with-me syndrome' which 'is not much help if he ain't all right with you' (quoted in Gillborn, 1991). The risk of such a response can prevent teachers sharing experiences and problems with their colleagues. In such circumstances 'teaching problems, if they are discussed at all, are explored among status equals or confined to relatively safe, depersonalised issues' (Hargreaves, 1980, p. 143).

In Reid School discipline is not an issue to be hidden away or discussed only within a small group of 'safe' colleagues:

> One of the things which I think often surprises new staff here is that people are prepared to share their anxieties and their worries ... It is not *sneered* at and looked down upon.
>
> *(Senior teacher)*

There is a strong sense of positive peer support in the school which encompasses all teaching staff and works via a series of mechanisms ranging from a formal school-wide 'on call' system to the most informal and apparently haphazard contacts between colleagues on corridors and in the staffroom. When these contacts are examined more closely, however, it becomes clear that they are all part of a complex pattern of supportive networks which interweave to sustain the teachers' morale and encourage constructive strategies for handling problems that arise.

The senior management team play a crucial role in the formal networks of peer support. Firstly, the headteacher and the rest of the management team emphasise the importance of good communication between colleagues. Hence, when the headteacher decides that an incident warrants a temporary (or permanent) exclusion, the whole staff are immediately informed at the next staff briefing (which takes place before the start of each school day). This is a very simple, but also highly effective strategy; before rumour and gossip have a chance to begin, the whole staff are told the situation regarding each new incident. In addition to its obvious information function, this routinely emphasises that all staff have a role to play regarding discipline and allows teachers to feed back important information. One morning during our fieldwork, for example, an excluded pupil had already been seen inside the school. The senior management learnt this from staff, decided upon appropriate action and were immediately able to advise staff what to do if they met the pupil.

A second formal mechanism of support for colleagues operates through an 'on-call' system. During each timetable slot an established member of staff (usually with pastoral or senior management responsibilities) is kept free to respond to any teacher's need for back-up or help. This system helps to combat the sense of isolation that teachers can feel when faced with a disciplinary problem which may force them to leave a class unattended – sometimes creating more problems. A newly appointed teacher drew our attention to the system:

> [An important] thing here is about the support structure for staff because there is always a member of the senior staff on call. So if you are having a problem you know that there is *somebody* who you can get hold of.

Many teachers mentioned the on-call system to us: they see it as highlighting the genuine willingness to help which is a strong feature of peer relations at Reid. Indeed, almost every teacher we interviewed stressed the importance of the support they received from colleagues.

Peer support is encouraged and sustained through a series of mechanisms which often grow from the actions of either senior management and/or teachers who have worked in the school for some time and who understand the special demands of 'teaching Marshall kids'. They try deliberately to create opportunities for dialogue about discipline without creating a threatening or hostile atmosphere. This approach is both reflected in, and supported by, the senior management team's high visibility around the school. The following quotation, for example, is taken from an interview with a teacher during their very first term in the school:

> The one main thing, the contrast between here and where I have worked before, is the fact that the senior staff are very much part of the staff as a whole, they are not a separate group that don't particularly inter-react. Just the simple fact that they will come and sit in the staffroom at lunch-time. They are always talking to anyone. I must

admit I have come from places where you don't see the head, for example, from one week's end to the next and certainly the deputies have their own offices and they don't venture out very often. But here there is definitely a lot of mixing. They are around and they are seen around.

Researcher: How is that a help?

Because you feel if you have got a problem you can discuss it with anybody and that they are concerned and they *will* take action ... I just happened to mention to one of the senior members of staff that, last lesson on a certain afternoon, the third year seem to be as high as kites and keeping them in their seats is as much as they can cope with. He said, 'Oh, I'm free then. Would it help if I wandered round and was seen about in the corridor?' They are always trying to help you.

As a 'newcomer' to the school this teacher received a great deal of informal support, and not only from senior colleagues. Partly because of the insular nature of the Marshall estate, the school presents particular problems for new members of staff – irrespective of whether they are probationers or experienced staff taking up promoted positions of responsibility. Issues such as discipline and classroom control are among the criteria by which pupils most often judge their teachers (see Woods, 1990). In Reid, however, newcomers experience an especially difficult initiation. As the headteacher notes:

One of the things one notices is that you have to undergo some sort of *entrance test* into the community and to be accepted by the community as an 'OK person'. Whereafter it doesn't matter who or what you are. But if you fail that test then your life is hell whether you are a professional or someone simply living on the estate.

This view is confirmed by pupils who, when asked how they treat new teachers, respond:

Barry: Not very well.

Steve: Give 'em a hard time. [laughs]

Jenny: We do though. [laughs] Like, we try 'em out to see how much stick they'll take ...

All candidates for teaching jobs are warned about the demands which the school makes of its staff. Many newcomers are nevertheless surprised by how often, over a period of several weeks, they are tested out by pupils. The following extract from our field notes gives an example of just one of the many incidents through which the pupils routinely test newcomers to the school:

Kevin has just threatened to 'batter' the girl sitting in front of him. Suddenly he leaps to his feet, as if to carry out his threat. The teacher is by his side and says something in a quiet voice. Kevin calls to his friend (Dave), 'Coming outside?'
Dave replies: 'Is Miss sending you out?'
Kevin: 'Yeah. Coming?'
Dave: 'Just let me finish these answers.'

[The teacher leaves the classroom with Kevin but returns alone – Kevin is placed in a neighbouring classroom with another group.]

About ten minutes later the group are working steadily when, without warning, Dave gets up and begins to walk slowly to the door – looking behind him at the teacher and grinning. As the teacher sees him, Dave starts to speak:
'Miss, I'm just going to help.'
Teacher (in a rising voice but not shouting): 'Don't be silly. Sit down.'
Dave smiles at his friends at the back of the room and returns to his seat.

On this occasion the teacher seems to have passed the test – she had demonstrated to the class that she was 'OK': she did not explode, nor did she ignore behaviour that the pupils knew she should not tolerate. Over time the testing process consists of numerous similar incidents – none so serious as to get the pupil into 'real trouble', but each one requiring the teacher to react to behaviour which is clearly inappropriate. Later, in interview, the teacher involved in this example confirmed that she had been warned about the testing process and felt that she was beginning to win through:

When you are a newcomer here you need all the help you can get. I think it seems to be fairly accepted in the school that the pupils look on you as fair game when you first start and they will only gradually start responding to you as they get to know you … I have noticed a change in a number of pupils' attitudes towards me …

Because the testing process is well known, new staff receive a very great deal of informal support from colleagues at all levels within the institution. Looking back on her probationary year one teacher recalls, 'It was literally like if you were walking down a corridor and somebody said, 'Are you all right? How's it going?' It was very haphazard but it was nice that way … '. The informal networks of support are not in fact as haphazard as many staff believe. In many cases senior and more experienced teachers deliberately use apparently routine or accidental meetings to provide an opportunity to talk and share experiences.

When teachers do confide in colleagues they usually receive a two-part response: firstly, they are assured that everyone in the school has experienced similar difficulties at one time or another: 'I've been here twenty years and I still have problems.' Secondly, they are encouraged to reflect on strategies which might help them to cope with the present situation and avoid similar problems in the future: 'It is *sharing* with members of staff the experiences that you have had … "this is what I did" and "this is what I tried" and "this is what I found worked … ".' The school has also begun to encourage teachers to observe each other in the classroom. At the time of our visit this was not systematised in any formal way, although several staff had enjoyed the opportunity to observe their colleagues (sometimes during INSET activities or as part of their work towards higher degrees). The benefits can be valuable, even for established and experienced members of staff.

Conclusions

In this chapter we have examined some of the ways in which an urban school has built and sustained shared professional commitment to key values amongst its staff. We are not arguing that the methods employed here can be simply transferred to other schools. Rather, the importance of the account lies in its exploration of how one institution has moved forward from a position of low morale, fragmented values and a highly stressed teaching force. It offers some ideas to teachers wishing to build a foundation for the development of consistent and positive relationships in schools.

The account points to the importance of making values explicit. The creation of a school 'values statement' served several purposes; it captured the strong, but previously tacit, sense of what the school was about and where staffs' priorities lay. Once agreed, the values statement provided a set of principles against which future developments and actions could be measured. It should not, of course, be assumed that beneath the surface of day-to-day doubts and conflicts every school staff shares certain fundamental core values (Ball, 1987). In this context, one way of providing a voice for differing viewpoints, and potentially resolving conflicts, is through the introduction of more democratic forms of management. Reid's success highlights some of the principles involved in encouraging staff to play a genuine part in policy formation and decision-making. In this way teachers are able to address differences in perspective and move toward greater consistency through the elaboration of key values to which they are professionally committed.

Whatever management style a headteacher adopts there is evidence that teachers place great value upon managers whom they can trust to keep them informed on matters of discipline. This is a key element in the building of trust between senior management and teachers. If this can be achieved in Reid (given the state of morale and management–teacher relations when the new head joined the school), one is tempted to speculate that it can be achieved almost anywhere. The school's progress highlights the importance of open and frequent communication between management and teachers.

4 Developing Dialogue

There are some young people in most schools who, for a variety of reasons, are not learning. Some of them routinely disrupt the learning of those they should be working with, or even threaten individuals whose school life then becomes troubled through fear and anxiety. The school whose work is the focus of this chapter, the Burran School, is putting its trust in 'dialogue' to help establish a platform of support and commitment from which it can more effectively tackle the wider issue of achievement.

Individual teachers in many schools commonly engage in dialogue, both in and outside the classroom. In the Burran School dialogue is not just something that particular teachers use in the privacy of their own educational philosophy but a co-ordinated feature of practices that are evolving within a whole-school framework of values. There is thus a continuity between individual teachers' informal use of talk and discussion and more formally structured opportunities for dialogue. The Elton Report (DES, 1989, pp. 240, 266–8) draws attention to this potential.

Dialogue signals a readiness to take seriously the views and status of others. It can make pupils feel that they matter as individuals – that there are adults who are taking the trouble to know them as 'unique ... , complex and distinctive' persons (Powell *et al*, 1985, p. 318). It can, consequently, help to build confidence and encourage some capacity for self-determination. Most significantly, perhaps, dialogue helps to assert a balance between rights and responsibilities. It enables the re-drawing of some of the power-relationships in schools that young people often experience as oppressive and which are usually mediated through bureaucratic exchanges. Bureaucratic discourse (see Rizvi and Kemmis, 1987, p. 289) is, conventionally, 'one directional' and privileges the words of those who are 'senior' by virtue of their being adult and teacher. As Gottlieb (1979, p. 437) explains, there are 'numerous ways in which people of different races, sexes and economic classes are socialised into taking unequal roles in a dialogue'. Thus, the opportunity to engage in genuine dialogue can give pupils some sense of self-worth in a world which may already be signalling that they are, in the words of Stevie Smith (1962, p. 91) 'Only one of many/ And of small account if any.'

Another strength is that dialogue enables teachers to recognise the emotion that young people who break the school's code of conduct are experiencing. As Furlong (1991, p. 296) has said, 'Even the most hardened pupils will experience intense and often contradictory emotions when they are challenging school. Feelings of anger, fear, frustration, elation and guilt may all be present.' For some, these feelings are 'a *product* of their educational experience; schools make all sorts of demands on pupils and for some this can result in "hidden injuries" that are the basis of disaffection'. For other pupils, school is not the primary cause of these turbulent emotions but merely a site where they give vent to feelings that have quite different roots: ' ... it is because school is so often a demanding experience that children who are already emotionally vulnerable choose to reject it.'

It follows that schools might aim to provide 'conditions that give students the opportunities to speak with their own voices' so that they can become aware 'of the dignity of their own perceptions' (Giroux, 1983, p. 203). This is an important aspiration for teachers and parents to have of young people for whom the future, in terms of employment and career, may well look bleak. What dialogue can offer is a language of possibility.

Interestingly, the Burran School's LEA has also come to appreciate the value of dialogue, in particular as a resource for parents and teachers in responding to problems of drug-taking and violence in the locality. For instance, a booklet on drugs offers parents clear and well-presented information and advice and concludes by urging parents to talk with their children:

> One long serious talk may not be enough. You should be ready to sit down and talk with them regularly. This is clearly the best way to share your worries about their health. Above all, *listen to what they have to say*.

DIMENSIONS OF DISCIPLINE

And the LEA's guidelines for dealing with harassment include the following passages:

[The teacher] attempts to understand the other person and his or her point of view – tries to recognise what it must feel like to be that other person living his or her life, and is aware of feelings or situations that resonate within him or her. This is an empathetic response and it is not the same as sympathy, which tends to be unhelpful … [Pupils] are not used to being really listened to in school and may feel uncomfortable and suspicious … Listen without interrupting and show you are interested and involved.

In the account that follows we look first at the school and its community and the ways in which parents are being brought into dialogue with the school about what it is trying to achieve. The central section describes the different arenas where dialogue between teachers and pupils is beginning to work and shows how the formal system of sanctions has been modified to reflect the values that dialogue represents. Overall, the account indicates the contribution of dialogue to ensuring that this is a school where respect for learning and respect for the individual combine to encourage achievement.

The Burran School

The last year that I attended this school was when it went comprehensive because previous to that it was girls one side and boys the other. And we had to call them Madam and we could only walk on one side of the corridor. The front door you could only use if you were a fifth year or a prefect.

The speaker is a parent in her early thirties and her child is now a pupil. It was in the 1970s that the school 'went comprehensive' and in the 1980s it became a community school. Had she not become closely involved with the school through being a mature student she would not have known how fundamentally it has changed and is still changing. The number of parents who have recent first-hand knowledge of what the new Burran is like is growing but the community has tended to let the school get on with its business without much 'interference' – but also without much support. Parental attitudes to schooling have ranged widely – from unconcern to full acceptance.

The school serves a predominantly white working-class community in a borough where people of ethnic minority background constitute about a quarter of the population. A comprehensive school four miles away has a 90 per cent black pupil population; the Burran School has an 80 per cent white population. The borough edges onto docklands and unemployment is high.

The retirement of a long-serving head was followed by two short-term appointments. The present head – who came from another tough school in the region – had been in the school 18 months at the time of our fieldwork – and seemed committed to staying. Her priority in her first year was to begin to rebuild the school's reputation in the eyes of the community and the LEA. Dialogue, as a foundation for good teacher–pupil relationships, features strongly (as we saw earlier) in the LEA's guidelines on dealing with drug problems, responding to incidents of harassment and enhancing achievement, and the head and various of her colleagues are in sympathy with such an approach which reflects their own personal and professional values.

Within the senior management team, for example, the deputy head who co-ordinates the pastoral work is a strong advocate of a dialogue-based approach and has tried to appoint heads of year who share his thinking. Another deputy head has extended the use of dialogue as a way of exploring situations in drama to her work on gender and sexual harassment. There are also a number of individual teachers who have an affinity for the values that underlie the approach, including those who have volunteered to serve on the anti-racist committee. However, a minority of staff – particularly those who have taught in this school for many years – have not changed their way of relating to pupils: they are still catching up with the school's new sense of confidence and its determination to abandon the old 'deficit model' thinking.

Indeed, to mark the end of her first year here, the head told the whole staff, in a carefully prepared review of the year, 'I don't ever again want to hear anything about "What can you expect from the kids from this area?" because we can expect the world!' The pastoral inspector for the LEA says that while he doesn't expect dramatic changes overnight, he is surprised at what has been achieved in this school in a relatively short time – once a majority of the staff started to pull together, once they had begun to believe that 'the school has something to offer', and once they had learned not to back-pedal on academic achievement but to build on the strengths of the pupils.

If the head's first priority on arriving was to enhance the school's general reputation and to begin to tackle low expectations among pupils, her next is to build strong links with parents. She will not say that the community has not been supportive – characteristically and strategically she adopts a positive stance; she prefers, instead, to say that there have in the past been too few opportunities for parents to express their support for the school and what it is striving to achieve for their children. Some large and influential families have lived in this community for genera- tions and their children have always attended the school on this site – even though absenteeism has been high and is sometimes encouraged by younger members of local gangs who, says the head, can resent the statu- tory power that the school has 'to command' attendance. Some people in the community have power 'as a family, or as individuals who have a name. They get their power from being able to threaten or to run the area in the way they see fit, which is not always the way that "decent" citizens would like it to be run' (headteacher). Teachers are not automatically regarded as powerful; they have to earn respect, and within such a cul- ture education has to seem important to parents and to pupils if they are to go along with it.

Becoming a community school has helped: parents who enrol as mature students, often working alongside pupils, value education for the second chance that it has given them and they then come to value it for their children. Even in an area of relatively high unemployment, they see how learning and qualifications can help you, in the end, to think highly of yourself and have some sense of purpose. (The relationship between Burran School and its community is explored further in chapter 6.)

The school cannot, of course, afford to rely only on the support and understanding of parents who are students, and it has recently found new ways of involving parents more directly in its purposes. A Parents' Group has been established which meets with the head twice a term. It is not concerned with fund-raising or similar activities. Its members are, at present, the 'active minority' but the head thinks that its membership will be extended and their influence could, in time, be considerable. The parents set their own agenda and recent discussions have focused on homework, English in the National Curriculum, information technology and uniform. The parents take responsibility, with secretarial help from the school, for consulting with and informing the parent body at large. Another development relates to the entry process: all Year 7 pupils are interviewed by the head or one of her senior colleagues and a parent or guardian must also be present. During the meeting, the school's aspirations for the pupil are discussed and all three sign a written 'Statement of Partnership' that records a tripartite awareness of and commitment to the school's policy:

The school will:

- keep parents informed of all school changes and developments;

- invite parents to be involved in decisions and discussions about the school;

- arrange regular meetings to discuss [the pupil's] progress;

- alert you to any difficulties as they appear;

- establish a code of behaviour to ensure a learning environment which is safe and caring.

Our experience suggests that there are ways in which you can demonstrate your interest in a valuable and supportive way by showing:

- a sympathetic understanding of the needs and concerns of [the pupil] while a pupil at school;

- an interest in [the pupil's] work and wherever possible taking an active part in supporting his or her study, particularly with homework;

- a willingness to take part in a two-way communication with school in order to keep up to date with [the pupil's] progress;

- a willingness to share any concerns about [the pupil's] health, education or behaviour;

- support for the school's code of behaviour;

- an interest in the wider community activities of the school.

The document (one side of A4) concludes with three signatures (for the school, the parents, the pupil) as witnesses to the acceptance of the 'Partnership'.

The school's approach is straightforward and supportive and expresses a concern to help pupils achieve something worthwhile. For instance, during the Easter vacation, when a number of pupils are regularly worried because revision has been left too late and/or because they do not have good conditions at home for undertaking concentrated study, teachers volunteer to come into school to give extra guidance and tuition. The school also puts a lot of effort into helping pupils who are truanting for periods of time ease themselves back into regular attendance. They are encouraged to come back for at least two or three mornings a week at first (the school regards partial attendance which the pupils value as better than total non-attendance). The returners are counselled individually during these morning sessions and are encouraged to talk about the things they like in school and are good at as well as the things they dislike; the things they enjoy and are good at out of school; and the subjects they like and the teachers they get on with. Individual schedules are then jointly designed which link a student with an activity and a person that they feel comfortable with and which allow them to build on their strengths. The concern is to help them feel that they are coming back into a climate that is supportive and in which they can have some sense of membership.

Some teachers feel that the school as a whole is perhaps too large for pupils to feel a global sense of membership and it is the year group that pupils are encouraged to identify with. Sport and the arts – which are enthusiastically supported by both pupils and the community – are reliable routes into shared commitment and shared enjoyment. The idea for a new options-based arts/sports course came from the pupils. They influenced its content and form and their sense of ownership (it is to be regularly reviewed so that successive year groups feel that they have a stake in it) seems to be positively influencing their commitment to it: 'Our attendance goes up – even for afternoon sessions. ... that's *one* way we measure relevance.' The course allows pupils to express something that comes 'from inside them – they just seem to be very good at it': it may be that they respond better to those areas of the curriculum where they have a talent that the curriculum allows them to develop rather than to areas where there are no obvious starting points in their own knowledge, interest or experience and where they become mere receivers of something that the school chooses to give them.

Staff take very seriously the aim of establishing security for all pupils: 'On the way to school, or on the way back to school or at lunch time. It is our responsibility. We are a community school.' Playground violence and within-school violence are beginning to decline, but the school has committed itself to sorting out the incidents that its pupils are involved in both inside and outside the school. Old wounds can easily be re-opened in settings where the watchful support of the school staff is absent. Dialogue with those involved does not always prevent a recurrence of aggressive behaviour, particularly where incidents are fed by racism or by other deep-rooted animosities; the local culture is one where personal vendetta can be a powerful influence on action. Nevertheless, the teachers see dialogue as the only way forward: punishment meted out in an authoritarian style has not proved effective and teachers want to try an alternative. They are clear what principles should guide interpersonal relationships and the head believes in making sure that the school's policy is explained and reinforced: 'This is what we stand for, this is what we believe in, this is what you knew when you came into the school' and parents are beginning to see that the school is trying to model, in its own relationships, the principles that it advocates for others: as one parent told us, 'In this school, if they say something, they act on it.'

Teachers at the school – described by an inspector as 'a very aware staff' – learn that they have to stay cool and avoid confrontation at

DIMENSIONS OF DISCIPLINE

all costs. They have benefited from some in-service work on the skills that dialogue draws on – careful listening and open questioning, for instance. Talking and listening are not easy skills to learn in a community that has valued action above words, and the school is developing a policy of establishing dialogue with parents as well as with pupils. The school feels that if parents are not working with them for the wellbeing of their children then progress will be superficial:

> You've got to make the parents realise what the school is trying to do. Unless they are involved and they are committed as well, when students go through the school gates it can all end. All you're doing is containing them in a building.

> *(Headteacher)*

The staff are beginning to believe that their efforts to communicate with parents will bear fruit in the long run and that the school and its community could work 'to the same agenda at the end of the day'.

Dialogue and Relationships between Teachers and Pupils

The staff want to help pupils think about their own capacity to understand and challenge situations that might otherwise be taken for granted: in particular, teachers are sometimes shocked at the readiness of 'victims' to accept their lot in life: 'They think they should just put up with it. They tolerate a lot' (teacher). Teachers see dialogue, or 'talking things through', as a way of helping those who are exploited by their peers be more self-reliant and also, for those pupils who are aggressive, as a way of trying to understand the problems that lie behind behaviours that bring them into conflict with teachers and with their peers.

Teachers also think it necessary to help pupils value the importance of explanation and justification in learning. In the present climate, the old strategy of saying, 'If you don't work hard you won't get a job' carries no weight because pupils know that even if you are well-qualified it is still difficult to build a career in the locality – and that even if you have no qualifications you can still earn 'a quick few quid'. Teachers try, therefore, against this discouraging backdrop, to help pupils take a more long-term perspective and understand that qualifications may offer them more flexible routes through life in the future.

Dialogue and the School's Formal Framework of Sanctions

A framework of sanctions operates within the school but some conventional features have been modified, where possible, to allow an opportunity for 'talking things through'. Disorderly and disturbing behaviours in the classroom are handled via supervised exclusions from lessons; all such exclusions are monitored by the head of year and parents are always informed so that they and the pupil concerned understand that it is a serious matter to behave inappropriately to others within the classroom. The school also uses detentions as a means of deterring persistent minor offenders and operates an 'on report' system – described by one pupil as 'a bit like being on bail'.

Serious incidents lead to the possibility of permanent exclusion which, for the head, is tantamount to acknowledging that the school has failed one of its pupils. It has, therefore, modified the procedures to reflect its wish to support the pupils who are in trouble and to help them to understand the reasons for their behaviour and the possible consequences. Before the proposal to exclude is finally made – exclusion, interestingly, is seen as 'abandonment' – the head will discuss with a pupil, in the presence of a parent or guardian, whether there is some task that they are prepared to engage in that they and the school would see as an appropriate commitment given the nature of their offence. If the pupil is, by then, ready to accept the need for a fundamental change of behaviour, then the terms of a 'contract' are discussed and written out by the pupil him- or herself and signed by the pupil, the parent/guardian and the head. It could say, for instance, that the pupil will do his or her utmost to be less aggressive every day for an agreed number of weeks and that the school in turn will arrange some mutually agreed constructive activity – for example, working one morning, each of those weeks, in a local nursery school. The contract is then typed and copies are signed by pupil, parent and the head: 'We are saying you can negotiate your own statement and we will back you on it. It really is still part of our "talking things through" – part of the same package' (headteacher). The head is offering a last chance: an opportunity for a pupil to pledge himself or herself to

54   DIMENSIONS OF DISCIPLINE

changing and monitoring their behaviour, and alongside this there is a task that must be reliably performed that is not only a way of atoning for what has been done but also a way of proving, in a different setting, a pupil's capacity for sustaining non-conflictual interpersonal relationships.

If permanent exclusion seems the only possible route, then the case is brought to the governors, who insist on knowing what support has been made available by external agencies and what support and counselling the pupil has had from teachers in the school.

Dialogue and the Year Heads' Pastoral Responsibility

The school's policy is for heads of year and form tutors to move with their pupils through the five years of secondary schooling and in this way to build a strong sense of understanding, support and 'membership' of the year group. Heads of year are often dealing, of course, with incidents that involve pupil–teacher confrontation as well as incidents between pupils.

One head of year explains how he values dialogue. First, the setting has to be right. His office is small and he decided to remove the desk, which took up most of the space, and to replace it with three small easy chairs and a rug. The room seems uncluttered and comfortable as a space to meet and talk in.

In responding to anti-social incidents involving a teacher and a pupil he will explore the facts of the situation and encourage the people involved to understand each other's perspective:

> I am of the opinion that there are two sides. I don't like the idea that the teacher is always right and the pupil is always wrong. So I do try to establish first of all that they have a right to say what has gone on – a version of the truth according to them. And I listen to that and I make notes on what they are saying.

Writing down what people say is a device for making them see that their accounts are being taken seriously and should not therefore be misrepresented. He tries to find out what the people involved in the incident were feeling and what led them to act in the way that they did; he encourages them to view the situation from the perspective of the other. If an agreed account of what took place is arrived at, and if the pupil proves to be at fault, then the teacher is invited to say what he or she thinks should happen and the next step is then explained to the pupil:

> Look. This is what we think. This is what we feel. This is why we are suggesting what we are suggesting. Usually I ask them, 'Do you think this is appropriate?' and if they think it is then I know we are round about right. They don't seem to lie and they don't seem to play any games.

If a teacher is at fault, then the code of the community – and increasingly of the school – expects an apology:

> What the parents are asking for is absolutely fair. It's that you would not accept this behaviour from my child so why does my child have to accept that sort of behaviour from the teacher. All they're asking is that the teacher says sorry to their son or daughter and I would say 90 per cent of our teachers do that. There are a few who still do not wish to ... Parents accept that children are difficult, they accept that teachers are human, but they also expect teachers to apologise if they've done wrong.

Dialogue and the School's Anti-Sexist Policy

Dialogue is a central feature of the approach used by a female deputy head (also a drama teacher) who is responsible for gender-related issues. In cases of reported harassment, she tries first to see the victim and to talk through what he or she thinks has happened. She will then see the aggressor and tell him or her what account of the incident she has had so far and ask the pupil for their view of the situation and their feelings. She then brings both victim and aggressor together. She thinks that the strategy works and the main indicator of its effectiveness is that the pairs or groups of children who have been involved in an incident tend not to repeat the behaviour. She also thinks that pupils see the strategy as both fair and firm:

Everybody gets a chance to say their piece. The children feel that I'm
not shouting at them, that I've given them a chance to talk. They have
a chance to tell me why – because there's always a reason – and how
they got themselves into that situation.

She concludes by asking each of them what they think should
happen:

Victims, most of the time, want either an apology or to be left alone . . .
They invariably want the person removed from their sight for a while
and if it's really serious I would do that. A lot of the time they're prepared to accept an apology so then I call the other person in, having
said to them, 'Right. They're being nice to you. They're prepared to
accept an apology. I've got to believe that you mean it.' So then they
come in and they sit here, we all sit together, and one says they're
sorry. And I say (to the victim): 'Well, do you want to say anything to
them? This is your chance. If you want to say, "You're a real sod for
doing that to me", you are in power here – You do it.' One particular
girl was receiving a lot of verbal abuse over a sexual attack that she
had suffered. The boys were mortified when they found out that what
they'd been shouting out turned out to be true. She was prepared to
accept an apology but she wanted to give them hell so I let her and
they had to sit there and listen. When she left I said to them, 'That's
how angry she feels, so never again.' And nothing's happened since.

She justifies allowing the complainant to express anger in terms
of their feeling some sense of power – 'Otherwise they feel just like a victim' – even after the apology has been made: 'So I think that's why it's
worth doing, even though it takes an afternoon.' She is critical of conventional institutional practice for dealing with boys' harassment of girls:
boys are often punished by men and 'it's like a boys' own club' where the
male teacher can say, in a 'buddy' style: 'Look. I don't really think there's
anything wrong in what you said but don't do it again for *me*. Okay?' She
adds: 'That can't happen here'. The appeal must be to a general principle
of respect which is there to guide the behaviour of all pupils and all
teachers.

Her concern is to rescue the victims of harassment from the sense that that is their role in life. Providing space for pupils to talk about their experience demonstrates that adults have respect for pupils as individuals and it can restore some self-confidence. It helps them to face up to situations, to open up about feelings, to explain and explore what might lie beneath the surface and to begin to take responsibility for their own actions towards others.

Dialogue and the School's Anti-Racist Committee

Disruptive incidents that are seen as an expression of racism are handled by a committee consisting of five members, each of whom is attached to one year group and whose responsibility it is carefully to record and follow up all incidents that are reported. In the case of aggressive behaviours, whether physical or verbal harassment, a member of the anti-racist committee will try to see the victim and the aggressor individually. The structure of the dialogue is similar to that reported above. To start, the committee member usually asks first for a statement of what happened. Feelings are then explored: how do you feel now? how do you think the other pupil feels? what do you feel about that person? At some point the pupils are reminded about the borough's policy and the school's policy.

The final stage in the dialogue is where each pupil is asked what he or she thinks should happen as a result of the incident and how they might be helped to avoid such incidents in the future. Where traditional authoritarian approaches to unacceptable behaviour would concentrate on punishing the aggressor, here teachers try to find out if there are any problems that pupils need help with or that may fuel a sustained desire to attack others.

Teachers acknowledge that in some situations they can make little progress: for instance, an aggressor may see a within-school incident as a legitimate outcome of a conflict that has nothing to do with the school or the teachers: 'I counselled someone the other week and he just wouldn't talk throughout the whole interview, just kept his head down and said, "It is nothing to do with you, nothing to do with you". And I didn't get through at all' (member of the anti-racist committee).

Sexual and racial harassment are not the only sources of distress. Pupils who choose not to wear, or are unable to afford, the clothes that are esteemed by the youth culture also suffer, as one pupil explains:

Like, people will see you wear certain clothes. Some people can't afford so much things. They might not be wearing designer shoes or something like that so you would get run [ie criticised] about that. And some people it afflicts them in a bad way because sometimes their parents haven't got much money and there is no control over that at the moment here. They haven't done nothing about that. ... The thing is, it is the way they say it. They can provoke you really bad by saying these things and then you'll have to strike them for saying what they're saying and you could get chucked out for that. (Year 10)

The school is in fact aware of the harassment and has recently sought advice from the Parents' Group (who conducted a survey) and from pupils. It has introduced an inexpensive basic uniform of prescribed tie and jersey, with black shoes and black skirt or trousers. These can all be cheaply bought in local shops or markets and allow pupils some choice of style.

While the existence of the anti-racist committee signals the school's attempt to take racial harassment seriously, having an opportunity to discuss an incident with a member of a committee is not as easy as discussing it with a teacher of your choice, whom you know and trust:

You see, a lot of people might not want to speak to [someone they don't know]. They might think that they can relate to somebody else a bit more easily. Other teachers, who I *think* I know better, I might want to talk to them about any problems that I might have. (Black pupil, year 10)

The same pupil acknowledges that the teachers at the school are generally 'all right':

I get on with all of them. There is not really a teacher that I don't get on with at this school. I can't say nothing bad about the teachers. ... I don't think I have come across a racist teacher. If they are racist then I don't really know about it because they don't behave racist towards the pupils. They are quite fair really.

At the same time, the pupils may be reluctant to take advantage of the opportunity for reporting incidents and talking about them for reasons other than their not knowing the particular member of the committee that is attached to their year. First, the local culture has strong conventions about tale-telling or 'grassing'. Second, pupils may be reluctant to acknowledge incidents in which they have been victimised because they take pride in a brand of macho toughness that is about 'taking it' and not getting someone else to sort out your problems for you. Third, some black pupils whom we spoke with were clearly sceptical of the school's capacity to deal effectively with racist attacks: what they have seen is the aggressor being excluded for a while and then returning: 'I have experienced some racism but I haven't really gone to report it because I don't really know what they would do would be good enough ... All they do is suspend them for a certain time and let them back in so they carry on doing it.' What is missing, from the pupil's perspective, is a sense that dialogue, used instead of or alongside exclusion, might be a way, with some pupils, of getting them to review their behaviour so that they don't 'carry on doing it'. Because he does not think he can rely on the school to take appropriate action, this pupil has developed his own coping strategy which is effectively self-protective in that it at least shifts the focus of the attack:

> The only way to get by that [ie racist name calling] is really to just laugh or ignore them or do it back or something like that ... If you walk away from them they call you even more names. If you just keep ignoring them they will think, 'Oh well' and leave you alone then. If you just ignore people then in the end you get on their nerves, not your nerves, and they will think, 'Oh leave him. He hasn't done anything about it. Go and put on someone else' and they just leave you alone.

The pupils also thought that one outcome of their peers becoming aware that the school had 'come down a bit strong about harassment, whether it's racial or to do with pupils' gender' was that the attacks were now being made 'in a more sly way'. They also recognise that however hard teachers in the school may try with some pupils, they won't win: 'Some of them don't care, they have got that type of attitude ... They think they are really untouchable.'

These pupils were uncertain – not surprisingly, perhaps – what to do when school work takes them outside the school gates and they come up against the structures and traditions that sustain racism in society at large. One black pupil recalled what happened in his recent work experience placement:

There is a manager ... and I was asking him a few questions ... I asked him a question about what type of person is best suited to the jobs here and he was telling me that the person has got to be white and everything like that. Everybody there was white and I noticed he was all chummy with the managing director so I didn't think there was nothing I could do.

The pupil commented, in a balanced way, that he didn't think anybody at school 'expected that to happen' but nevertheless he didn't report it. Instead, he told his parents and his father phoned the school: 'I think they might be taking it further', he said. The enquiry that followed concluded with a letter of apology from the manager to the pupil concerned. There was also a very positive general outcome. A youth worker from the on-site Youth Centre and a colleague from the Adult Education Centre counselled the pupil (both were well known to the pupils through their involvement in leisure activities) and, seeing what deep distress he had suffered, set up, with the head's support, a 'young black persons group' where pupils can talk through, in school hours, anxieties, fears and difficult experiences.

Pupils know that teachers are committed to supporting them and to eradicating racial harassment but they also know that the attacks they experience as pupils are fed by powerful forces outside the school. Exclusions provide a cooling-off period – not a cure. What the school hopes is that in the medium to long–term the coherence of its values, the firmness of its stance on violence, and its use of dialogue in particular situations will begin to have some impact on the attitudes of pupils who behave aggressively. Progress may be slow but there is evidence that both pupils and parents are beginning to understand the school's position on harassment and aggression and on the need for people to respect and support each other if all are to have the opportunity to learn.

Conclusions

The Burran School is one of many schools that are trying to give more prominence to dialogue within their framework of support for learning. In some schools dialogue may be used primarily in situations where codes of inter-personal and institutional behaviour are broken and other people are consequently hurt or upset. In others it may be used more in counselling situations where pupils become isolated, depressed or withdrawn because they are not coping with the demands on their lives. It may be used in curriculum-related ways where dialogue helps pupils to recognise purpose and individual progress in learning (as in the school whose work is discussed in the next chapter), and it may have a place in evaluative situations where opportunities are made for pupils to review school experiences critically, constructively and often collaboratively. And there may be some schools which are trying to build a coherent, whole-school framework in which dialogue is central to developments in several of these areas.

At the Burran School, dialogue is a key feature of the school's attempts to create a climate and relationships that underline its pupils' right to learn. So far the school has introduced dialogue across various aspects of its 'disciplinary' structure, making it positive in spirit and regenerative. This development is complemented by efforts to help parents understand the school's thinking and its aspiration for its pupils.

What can we learn from the Burran School's experience? First, our interviews suggest that it is important for teachers to find ways of tuning in to pupils' sub-cultures. They may need, for example, to know more about the problems pupils have in reporting incidents that break the school's code of conduct, and what kind of incident pupils would feel justified in reporting because, perhaps, their sense of fairness in some circumstances is stronger than their dislike of 'grassing'. And if teachers are to monitor the impact of dialogue on the incidence of aggressive behaviour, they need to know whether bullying or harassment is actually decreasing or whether, as some pupils say, it is merely less explicit, taking a different form.

The Burran experience confirms that it is important that every pupil in the school feels that there is a teacher that he or she can turn to for advice and help. Interestingly, this is one of the three performance indicators proposed by Gray (1990) in his discussion of the quality of schooling:

Academic progress: What proportion of pupils in the school have made above-average levels of progress over the relevant time period?
Pupil satisfaction: What proportion of pupils in the school are satisfied with the education they are receiving?
Pupil–teacher relationships: What proportion of pupils in the school have a good or 'vital' relationship with one or more teachers?

In relation to the third indicator, Gray and Jesson (1990) comment that while many teachers talk about good relationships, 'It is apparently difficult to be particularly tangible or specific' and they go on: 'it stikes us as a nettle to be grasped, whatever the difficulties it may initially pose'. The Burran School has grasped the nettle – and would claim that 'dialogue' is a key component of good relationships between teachers and pupils.

A second set of issues relates to the language in which dialogue is conducted. We know that in situations where teachers provide opportunities for pupils to look critically and constructively at particular lessons or teaching and learning styles, they need to find ways of helping pupils to acquire 'a language of critique' (see Cowie and Rudduck, 1989). Here, at the Burran School, it would be helpful to know whether pupils sometimes – or often – feel 'lost for words' – the words that allow them to express the complex emotions that they might be experiencing. This is a potentially important area, for if pupils are able to articulate certain feelings they are more likely to be able to confront and reflect on the behaviours that are being driven by those feelings.

Finally, before concluding this account, we should confront the well-documented criticism of 'regenerative' approaches – such as the use of dialogue in the Burran School – which are powerful in their use of empathy. The criticism is that such approaches 'incorporate' or 'co-opt' pupils into an institutional (usually middle-class) value system. Furlong

(1991, p. 301) offers a helpful summary of this position. Through our power, as teachers, the criticism runs:

> We attempt to get children to accept certain values, to aspire to certain futures for themselves and to accept and understand their own strengths and limitations. Educational structures ... [are] used not just to impose certain sorts of behaviour but to construct young people in particular ways. We do not use our power simply to force children to act in these ways. Rather we insist that they come to see themselves and organise their lives in these ways.

The concern expressed in the quotation is that schools may subtly be taking away the right of pupils to make a justifiable response to what they experience, sometimes out of school and sometimes inside school, as the prejudice and narrow-mindedness of the system. David Hargreaves (1982) has already documented the loss of dignity which certain forms of schooling can inflict on young people and it follows that protest can, in such a context, be construed as a rational response. Teachers at the Burran School might well agree but they would want to add that any act which damages others or undermines their right to learn is an affront to the set of commonly held educational values – respect for others and non-violence – that the school is trying to reflect in its practices and relationships. They might also say that the school has confronted and acknowledged its own 'institutional culpability' (Apple, 1990, p. 134) for at least part of the problem of motivating its pupils, and that it is trying, in a concerted fashion, to make appropriate changes. Teachers could also say, with confidence, that dialogue is a way of helping pupils learn how, at some level, they can contribute to the task of 'remaking a dangerous and disordered world'.

5 Increasing Pupil Engagement

Educationists have increasingly argued for changes which enable pupils to adopt a more active role in their education. At a national level a desire to increase motivation by improving pupils' sense of achievement and 'ownership' of their work has been particularly prominent (McGuff, 1990). At the local level, individual schools have adopted a variety of approaches which share the goal of improving motivation and commitment to learning by increasing pupils' active participation in the educational process. In this chapter we concentrate on changes in one such school.

Seaview School has instigated a series of fundamental changes which acknowledge pupils' rights and actively involve them in assessment processes. The overall aim has been to increase pupils' involvement in their own learning, helping them to recognise their potential and increase their commitment to achieve. The changes have had far-reaching effects in the school, altering the basis of teacher–pupil relationships and, in some teachers' eyes, challenging their traditional claims to authority. The chapter is organised in two parts: the first deals with the changes in assessment procedures, outlining how the school's system works and is experienced by pupils; in the second the focus shifts to teachers. In particular, we examine how teachers have experienced the changes and the consequences for discipline.

Seaview School: Bringing Pupils Back In

Urban schools often face particular problems: their economic and social context can make schooling seem meaningless to a large proportion of pupils. Local unemployment, for example, can leave educational certification with little apparent value. School competes with a variety of activities which may offer more substantial rewards in the short term. In many cases pupils find alternative ways of passing the time, some of which lead them (as victims or perpetrators) to petty (and not so petty) crime. Although it does not fit the stereotypical image of an inner-city school,

Seaview faces all the motivational problems which one might expect in more economically disadvantaged areas.

Seaview serves the inner area of a large coastal resort. There is little in the way of local manufacturing industry and so the majority of working people are economically dependent on the tourist trade. The area is characterised by high geographical mobility: the availability of seasonal work, for example, attracts many families who otherwise rely on state benefit for all or most of their income. The holiday trade is always hungry for menial labour; hence, pupils know that there is 'easy money' to be made irrespective of age or educational achievement. Although the money is, in fact, anything but easy, it is a tangible alternative to study – one which proves increasingly attractive to many pupils as they near the end of their compulsory schooling.

Seaview, therefore, shares many of the problems facing more conventionally 'urban' schools. Importantly, however, the school has refused to sit back and assume that improvement would be thwarted by external circumstances. Over recent years a concerted attempt, involving both staff and pupils, has been made to redefine the ways in which people work together in the school. One of the most striking changes has been a conscious drive towards greater involvement of pupils – involvement, not as the passive subjects of teachers' instructions and recipients of others' wisdom, but as active participants in the learning process. The headteacher's avowed aim is to 'empower' the pupils as participants, with rights and responsibilities, who recognise their own potential and are committed to success within the school. In an early planning document, written and submitted for whole-staff discussion, the headteacher summarised his aims as:

> a working practice based on openness, trust and partnership. All our practices must reaffirm the partnership and the right of pupils to a voice. This enfranchisement of the pupils must enhance their feeling of self-worth and will consequently improve motivation and performance.

The head's proposals encompassed the whole operation of the school; they were not limited solely to issues of discipline and good behaviour. The proposal did, however, acknowledge a shared awareness of worsening alienation and conflict within the school. A teacher who has worked there over the last decade describes the situation as follows:

> It is becoming increasingly difficult for those [teachers] who got away with ... 'You tell them what to do because *you* say so'... A lot got away with it when I was at school by all sorts of bluff and mystique. A lot got away with it when I started teaching. But the number getting away with it is getting less and less.

During the 1980s, the need to earn respect and to justify authority became increasingly plain in Seaview. The headteacher's proposed philosophy for the school (which was accepted by staff at a training day on future development) is based on the view that schools can play an active role in the creation of good working relationships and pupil motivation. As the headteacher noted during interview:

> The *vast* majority [of schools] still keep children at that level of subservience which is common to our society... I cannot see that we can continue to do that and succeed. We *have* to find ways of addressing the growing disaffection and disruption... I think we have had to recognise that *we*, to a considerable part, are in fact causing it.

In order to consolidate the move from the realm of theory to practice, the head appointed a 'steering group' whose role was to oversee and implement practical developments which reflected the agreed philosophy. The steering group comprised staff of all levels of responsibility and filling a range of key pastoral and academic posts. Although the group started with relatively modest targets, such as the introduction of a Record of Achievement (RoA), the changes have in fact led to a fundamental shift in teacher–pupil relationships.

The Role of Assessment

Many school pupils feel at their most exposed, their most powerless, when they are being assessed. Historically, assessment and testing are associated with formal examinations, conducted in silence, where pupils must answer questions that are set and judged by someone else (an adult) who defines what is important and what is acceptable. This rather narrow view of assessment, of course, does not reflect the variety of ways in which teachers routinely judge pupils' achievements without resort to particular activities which we would recognise as 'tests'. Nevertheless, a good deal of work in schools is still patterned according to the assumption that assessment is something which is done *by* teachers, *to* pupils – casting children in the role of passive recipients. Hence, assessment can have particularly negative connotations: it risks labelling pupils as 'failures' whilst reinforcing the massive inequalities of power between teachers and pupils (Rudduck, 1991, p. 39).

In view of these problems, many academics and practitioners have long argued the need to integrate assessment as a positive aspect of pupils' school experience. In the UK it has been argued that the development of a comprehensive RoA, for example, has the fundamental purpose of 'raising students' sense of ownership and control of their own progress and, with it, their motivation, their sense of achievement and their self-esteem' (Broadfoot *et al*, 1991, p. 76). For its realisation, however, such a goal relies on the *process* by which RoAs should be produced – the physical form of the summative record itself (the product) is relatively unimportant. The Pilot Records of Achievement in Schools Evaluation (PRAISE) team, for example, opposed the view in which 'RoAs came to be envisaged as simply the vehicle in which curriculum successes are recorded – and little more'. They argued for:

> The more liberal comprehensive interpretation of RoAs in which students have a significant degree of 'ownership' of the learning process, in that they are encouraged to set personal goals and record progress towards them within and beyond formal curriculum provision.

(Broadfoot et al, 1991, p. 78)

When a format for the 'National Record of Achievement' was first published (DE/DES, 1991) some critics dismissed it as 'less a record of achievement and more like a glorified school report' (Nash, 1991). Nevertheless, the documentation which accompanies the National Record retains a commitment to a process of dialogue which seeks the pupil's active, and positive, participation: 'These processes of negotiation, review and planning involving both learner and teacher/trainer must underpin the development of Records of Achievement' (DE, 1991, para. 3). An approach to assessment which includes a significant role for the pupil, therefore, continues to draw support from several quarters. Beyond the rhetoric, however, many tensions still exist between perspectives which conceptualise assessment in terms of product and those which conceptualise it in terms of process. One of the difficulties may be a lack of clarity in some approaches which present the process model rather idealistically and without reference to concrete examples. This was certainly an issue which emerged in Seaview as the school began to rethink its approach to assessment during the late 1980s and early 1990s. The experiences of teachers and pupils in the school graphically demonstrate the problems but also indicate opportunities for greater participation and enhanced motivation.

The changes at Seaview were inspired by an intention to integrate assessment into the learning process. The head and steering group wanted to dismantle the traditional approach which they felt simply used assessment as an 'add-on' – something which was primarily reserved for specific points in the school year when pupils would be tested, ranked and informed of their progress (or lack of it), often through the briefest of comments on a simple 'report' sheet. As a head of department notes, 'I have filled in those A4 sheets, where you have a little bit of a line to put your comment, and it is the easiest thing in the world ... And it is quite meaningless.'

The attempt to make assessment more meaningful has meant opening up the assessment procedure. Assessment became a more frequent part of school life, but also a more dynamic and enjoyable one. Fundamentally, assessment has moved outside the exclusive realm of teachers and become the focus of dialogue between teachers and pupils – dialogue premised on the need for negotiation. The following passage is taken from an interview with Year 7 pupils:

Linda: If you don't agree with [the teacher's assessment] you don't sign it. You tell him and you sit down and he will explain it. And you have got to explain it to him, what you don't feel is right ...

Researcher:	What happens if you disagree with what [the teacher] has said? Do you have to go with their view?
Linda:	No. You talk through it and make some agreement in the end.
Sue:	You make a comment, don't you?
Linda:	He will make an agreement with you and then he'll go on the computer [where some assessments are recorded] and change it for you – if he agrees with what you've said.
Sue:	You have got to agree with each other, that's what happens, you have to agree with each of you.
Tracey:	And you have to be truthful as well.

Although these pupils had spent less than six months in the school, when interviewed they were already comfortable with both the principles and the mechanics of assessment. The principles concern the need actively to involve pupils; not simply telling them how they have achieved in the teachers' eyes, but including them in the identification of success and the setting of future targets. For this to be genuine, pupils must have the right to disagree. As Joanne (a Year 10 pupil) notes, the key difference between Seaview and her previous school is that she now has a voice in her own assessment:

> You both sign it. It is better that way because then you both get a say. A [traditional] report, you just get 'Oh, right. That's your marks, that's your comment and that's it'.

In the upper school (Years 10 and 11) assessment relates to the patterns of GCSE and TVEI work which pupils undertake as they move towards qualifications in external examinations. By this point in their school lives, the pupils are confident in the assumption that feedback will be frequent, and that assessment will be based on a shared perspective

70

agreed through negotiation. This situation is founded upon the explicit processes which pupils encounter in the lower school (Years 7 to 9). Here negotiations are focused around what can, at first, seem a bewildering array of different assessment procedures and instruments. Most prominent are:

- profiles
- attitudinal grids
- twice-yearly reviews.

The latter take a broad perspective covering the whole of a pupil's experience of school; profiles and grids focus on explicit parts of each subject area.

Profiles

In the lower school each subject department presents the curriculum through theme-based blocks of work lasting between eight and ten weeks. Each of these 'units' is accompanied by written guides which outline the tasks to be worked through and suggest a variety of resources which pupils might call upon. Although units in some subject departments follow a different physical format (sometimes as a series of worksheets, sometimes as a single booklet), every unit is read and 'accredited' by members of the steering group. The steering group check for a range of factors including accessibility of language, cross-curricular coverage, equal opportunities issues and the provision of extension work (for the more able) which represents a natural development of the unit. In addition, the steering group require each unit to begin by specifying its aims and objectives in terms of skills and concepts which the pupil will understand. There should be clear guidance about how the work is to be assessed. Although the units are made up of a succession of tasks, the introduction should make clear which elements will be carried forward to the pupil's RoA (should the pupil wish to include them); these might include an end of unit test or a series of key exercises which appear in the unit itself.

As a group nears the end of a unit, pupils meet individually with the teacher (for around ten minutes) to discuss their progress. The discussion considers both the learning which has taken place and the way in which the pupil has approached her or his work. The former is summarised in a written 'profile' which states the kind of work which has been completed and reflects positively on the pupil's achievements. This is written by the teacher and offers an authoritative account of progress during the unit. Although the profile will record problems and areas of concern, the overall tone should be positive, recognising achievement and encouraging the pupil to see improvement as a reachable goal.

To the pupils, profiles represent 'what the teacher thinks you have done through the whole course of that unit' (Year 7 pupil). Although teachers try to strike a balance between acknowledging progress and highlighting areas for future attention, profiles can, of course, sometimes make unwelcome reading. In pupils' eyes, however, even a disappointing profile is not equivalent to a 'poor report', which traditionally might have cast a shadow over an entire year's work. Profiles are never wholly critical: they offer constructive ways forward which relate to detailed points of the work under consideration and, significantly, their frequency offers pupils the chance of improvement in the short term (which will be recognised in the next profile). This point was made strongly by a Year 10 pupil who contrasted profiles with the more traditional end of year report format:

> You don't get them like at the end of every year, you get them every unit. You do a unit and you get an assessment at the end... and say, if it is bad, you think, 'Right, I have got to try better next time, revise more'. But at the end of the year you can't change the *whole* year can you? Because you have just got it at the end you don't get chance to change. But this, you can see where you are going wrong or how well you are doing.

This statement is deceptively simple. The pupil is discussing more than the mere frequency of assessment in the school; she is displaying a sense of control regarding her own learning; she is confident that if things go wrong ('if it is bad') she will find out before it is too late and will have the opportunity to improve.

Attitudinal Grids

Like profiles, *attitudinal grids* are completed at the end of each unit. Unlike profiles, however, these refer specifically to the pupil's attitude – the way in which they have worked rather than the outcomes they have achieved. Despite their somewhat over-elaborate title, the grids are simple devices used to encourage dialogue between teacher and pupil.

Although the content has remained fairly stable, the precise form of the grids has changed over time, building on the strengths and weaknesses identified by successive cohorts of Seaview pupils. When we studied the school, two main varieties were in use, both of which include a graphical presentation to summarise how well the pupil has worked. The first variety, used in Years 7 and 8, are known as 'bullseyes'.

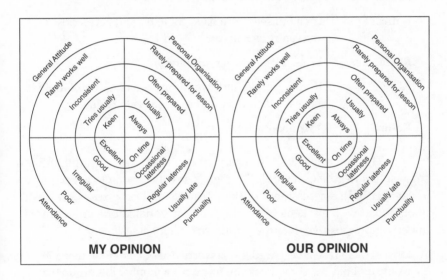

By shading in the relevant area pupils signify how well they have performed – on the basis of their own perceptions and as the result of discussions with the teacher. In Year 9 bullseyes are replaced by 'thermometer' style charts which allow pupils a little more subtlety when considering their answers to questions about punctuality, attendance, preparation and work in class.

The instruments themselves are very simple; their strength lies in the dialogue which they generate between pupil and teacher. This is a dialogue premised on the assumption that both parties must agree; they must discuss their views, put their own case and reach a final statement to which both are happy to lend their signature.

Researcher:	Do you get confused with all the different pieces of paper?
All:	No.
Katie:	[opening her RoA to show examples] We know what we've got; our review, our attitudinal grids ... So we file them in subjects.
Researcher:	What's an 'attitudinal grid'?
Katie:	It's a bullseye. You have got to try and get as close to the centre as you can.
Researcher:	What if [the teacher] disagrees?
Rich:	If you are like far away from agreeing, you would have a talk and try and sort something out.
Katie:	Talk about it.

This interview with a group of confident year 7 pupils might suggest that negotiation would frequently involve trying to get pupils to lower their initial assessment of their attitude and progress – yet this is not the case. Staff are keen to point out that negotiated outcomes are frequently more positive than the pupils' first (solo) assessments:

Most of them take it very well. I was worried about it at first, that a lot would quibble. But sometimes you find quite a number in a group that *under*estimate themselves. It works both ways; some that overestimate and some that underestimate.

Seaview teachers are aware that some pupils (especially the younger ones) need help and encouragement before they will take advantage of the opportunity to negotiate; a teacher in his first year at the school notes that some pupils are surprised when their opinions are sought – 'Well, it's not my place to discuss it with you'. Although such views are common among pupils when they enter the school, the principles of negotiation through dialogue are reinforced daily, and extend to the ways in which the school reports progress to the pupils' parents.

The Review Process

Subject teachers pass completed profiles and grids on to each pupil's form teacher. As a new teacher to the school explains, the frequent receipt of up-to-date information on each pupil's progress and attitude helps to keep tutors informed, alerting them to any signs that a pupil is having difficulties:

> The actual tutor side of it is quite easy because you get maybe ten [profiles] a day in your pigeon hole and you can glance through those quite quickly... I check that nothing's going wrong. If there is I take them aside and say, 'Look, what's going on in Physics?' Find out what the problem is...

> The Year 7 students have only been in the school ten or twelve weeks and there are pages starting to take shape [in the RoAs] – a number of them have taken them home and shown their parents what is going on. They really have taken to it very, very well. They are all saying to me, 'I have signed my science unit on Friday. Has it come through yet?' They are looking forward to them coming through.

The form tutor's routine involvement in the assessment procedure ensures that he or she is kept informed throughout the year. This relatively simple device helps to avoid the situation where tutors get information about academic and behavioural progress through classroom and/or staffroom gossip rather than the more formal channels (see Gillborn, 1991; Hammersley, 1984). In addition, twice a year Seaview form tutors take a central role in the assessment procedures through their involvement in the 'review' process.

Although pupils may take their RoAs home at any time, the school also arranges more formal 'review evenings' when RoAs are discussed. The review process begins over a two- or three-week period during which form tutors see each pupil individually (for around 15–20 minutes) to discuss their progress since the last review. As with the procedures for profiles and grids, reviews are carried out on a one-to-one basis and stress the importance of dialogue leading to the creation of a summative statement (in most cases written or word-processed by the pupil) and signed by both pupil and tutor. Once again the process encourages pupils to be both confident and honest. The following, for example, is a selection of entries taken from the review sheet of aYear 10 pupil:

Personal qualities/achievements

My attendance has been affected by hospital treatment and convalescence but my punctuality is excellent.

Communication

I can write clearly. I can produce accurate plans, maps and graphs as can be seen in my geography work. I can talk comfortably to adults.

Self-management/organisation

My planning of work needs improvement. When I was absent I did not keep up with the work sent home. It took me a long time to catch up and I am still just behind in English. I am managing to work on my geography fieldwork.

In common with so much of the Seaview system, the review process asks a great deal of teachers, who are expected to make time to see each pupil individually. Although the time schedule is demanding, staff support for the review system – especially the review evenings – is strong.

The pivotal role which form tutors play in helping pupils to collate and store their various assessments has allowed Seaview, in the lower school, to move away from a 'carousel' approach to parents' evenings. The staff who were initially most closely involved in introducing the assessment and curricular changes decided that the school's philosophical position (emphasising dialogue and pupil engagement) was not reflected in the brief conversations which parents managed to snatch as they moved from one subject specialist to another. Hence, the year group that first introduced negotiated assessments also tried a new approach to 'review evenings', asking parents to make an appointment to see the form tutor only. This was intended to generate a more meaningful discussion which would involve the pupil ('no student: no discussion'), and focus on the RoA, with the recently completed review statement as an overall guide to progress.

In order to give each pupil a 15–20 minute slot the tutors found themselves seeing parents over a six-hour period (between three in the afternoon and nine o'clock at night). The first team's experience proved so powerful that successive pastoral teams have followed their example. One of the original team describes the development as follows:

> [The headteacher] has never talked about directed time and nobody has brought it up. Because the feedback from those first two reviews was so incredible – we were getting 90-odd per cent attendance from parents, which we had never had in this place before – even the most cynical of tutors were coming out saying, 'Well, that was incredible'.

The improvement in parental attendance at review evenings is one of the achievements which Seaview teachers are most proud of. To achieve near total attendance, from a situation where only a minority of parents were regular attenders, is a very significant change – one which staff attribute to the improved atmosphere of genuine discussion and involvement. Certainly it is a change to which pupils report very positive reactions. A Year 10 pupil stated:

> *You* can ask questions, your mum can ask or your dad can ask. And the form teacher can ask. It's much better than having just a report because you get to *talk* about things.

The improved dialogue with parents has also led to changes in the kinds of issue which parents now feel able to raise with tutors. Although some staff have been taken by surprise, most appear to view the development as a positive step, one which, although challenging, can be used constructively by the school and which highlights the parents' active concern for their children's education:

> [The parents] are so much more relaxed. They have seen that same form tutor again and again, they are not so slow in coming forward . . .

So our parents are now far more articulate in what they want to know and what they want to say... That created a tension as well, as you can imagine, when you got to your second or third review evening and they would just say, 'Look. I am not very happy about what is happening in a certain subject...'

Just as the introduction of review evenings has changed the nature of the teacher–parent relationship, so teacher–pupil relationships have been affected by the other changes in assessment and the role of pupils in the school. The following section examines these changes more closely.

Coming to Terms with Changed Relationships

The school's new philosophy emphasises the need for dialogue between pupils and teachers. A positive and constructive approach is encouraged. As we have seen, in terms of assessment this view is reflected in new approaches to pupil profiling, curriculum delivery (through discrete 'units') and regular reviews which stress achievement and target setting. These are significant changes which fundamentally challenge some teachers' basic assumptions about their own role and authority.

When the moves toward greater dialogue and negotiation were first mooted to staff a common reaction was to stress how time-consuming it might be. In addition, some teachers felt that such a strategy might actually work against the pupils' interests by giving them false expectations of the world beyond the school walls. In some cases a powerful social deficit model emerged: Seaview teachers were not united in the view that their pupils were 'capable' of assuming the responsibilities which the changes would place upon them. The following extract, for example, is taken from an 'evaluation report' which describes the concerns which were expressed (during small group discussions) when the headteacher's initiatives were first given serious whole-school attention.

The question was asked, 'Might we not be doing children a disservice?' – by leading them to expect that the world outside would approach unacceptable behaviour in the same way as their school had done. It was felt by some members that there were some children who would either refuse to negotiate strategies for their own behaviour-modification, or who would simply be incapable of doing so. 'What happens then?' was the question asked. 'Nothing?' – or would we then have to abandon our philosophy and impose a sanction?

One colleague raised the example of chewing. Simple enough, it may appear, but might not negotiation lead to –

'Well, why can't I chew?'

'Because it's unpleasant – bad manners – unhealthy.'

'But everyone does it.' 'No one else minds.' 'It helps me concentrate', etc.

The fear was that, on many similar issues, inordinate amounts of time could be spent disagreeing with children on issues where we could not (ought not to?) give ground.

The notion that the imposition of 'a sanction' would require teachers to 'abandon our philosophy' is an especially complex issue which is only now (in the fourth year of the changes) becoming clear to the majority of teachers. The fear that pupils would be unwilling and/or incapable of sensible negotiation has also proved especially difficult to overcome. In fact this concern has been most effectively answered through the actions of teachers who have tried to put the ideals into practice. What has happened in the school, as we have already seen in the pupils' accounts of the assessment process, is that by and large the pupils have welcomed the greater degree of trust and responsibility which has now entered teacher–pupil interactions. The teachers have seen, initially through the example of committed colleagues, that pupils do not try to argue over trivial matters (such as chewing). Overall, the pupils' response has impressed many teachers who were originally very worried about the practicalities of negotiation.

The following example is from a teacher who was initially sceptical about how negotiation could deal adequately with serious disciplinary issues (in this case being told to 'Fuck off' in front of a class of sixteen-year-olds). She found, however, that, far from appearing weak, her readiness to negotiate gave her an opportunity to explain her position to the pupil and to gauge how best to proceed:

[At the end of the lesson the teacher took the pupil to see one of the deputy headteachers.] In the boy's favour I said how perfect he had been all lesson but then, because I'd insisted he did something, he just swore at me right across the classroom, and how disappointed I was. The boy was stood there, I said it in front of him, and I said, 'That's right isn't it, Roy?' I said, 'You didn't say anything more, so that was in your favour. It was just one insult that everybody heard.'

After a discussion it was decided not to contact the pupil's parents on this occasion; it was made clear that such an outburst could not be tolerated and would be dealt with more harshly if the same thing happened again. The incident was handled in a way which allowed the pupil to regain his composure and work through the consequences of his actions. Importantly, the pupil was not faced with an automatic process of escalating sanctions and control which could not respond to the particular circumstances of the incident – a situation which would have destroyed months of progress on his part:

We let him play a part in assessing whether it was right or wrong and what should be done and what shouldn't. He was quite calm and quite sorry... I think he had said it almost thinking he was at home or on the street – how they speak to each other sometimes – and before he knew where he was it had slipped out.

The teacher was confident that the pupil had learned from the episode and was pleased that a recent improvement in his behaviour had not been destroyed by a single lapse. She also recognised an important change in her own confidence about disciplinary issues and her ability to negotiate: 'At one time I probably would have gone in and said, "This boy has just told me to F. off. I insist that you do something – I am not having that".'

In this case the teacher had worked with the new approaches and found them to be successful. Some teachers, however, took a rather different view: to them, negotiation was a time-consuming nonsense which merely allowed pupils to get away with things unpunished:

The previous head was a strict disciplinarian but now you can't take action if kids do anything wrong.

Nowadays you have got kids telling people to 'F. off' – in the old days they would be expelled: you do something like that, you go. But now there is lots of talk; [in a soft, somewhat patronizing tone] 'Why did you say that?', that kind of thing. Nowadays you have to say it about three times before any action is taken. It's all very drawn out, it takes a lot more time. The process is a lot more involved and it is a lot more stressful.

Such teachers are critical of the whole philosophy underlying the attempt to heighten pupil engagement in Seaview. The idea of actively involving pupils in assessment and disciplinary issues runs directly contrary to some teachers' notions of proper power and authority within school. In interview, for example, a teacher objected to the fact that Seaview pupils own their RoA and decide which assessments and profiles to include. Although this has presented no problems in practice, the teacher objected to the principle, and to the 'whole attitude' underlying it:

If the child doesn't want their parents to see what we have written they won't see it. It is all up to the child – can you believe that? If the child doesn't want their parents to see it, that's it; they don't see it. It is this whole attitude. It is the parents' right to see the child's work but they can't see it unless the child says 'yes'. Now they [supporters of the changes] always say, 'No-one has ever refused for their parents to see the things', but that is not the point. It is this whole attitude...

In their turn, the teachers who were most committed to the changes responded to the criticism by feeling that some colleagues were refusing to give the innovations a chance:

The biggest problem for me – if I am being perfectly honest – is certain members of staff who have seized the opportunity of, in a way, misinterpreting what they think the head was all about and opting out. Saying comments like, 'Well, I informed the student's tutor and that is it, I can't do any more than that because otherwise I am going against the philosophy', or 'We can't do anything without the students' permission', which is rubbish.

Several of the most vehement critics of the moves toward greater pupil engagement chose to leave the school and, slowly, the new approaches have won credibility as teachers have seen (and experienced) them in action. Hence, Seaview teachers have increasingly realised that their early fears were largely unfounded. As one teacher told us, 'I am something of an old-fashioned teacher myself and I was against, not the practice, but what I understood to be the philosophy behind it ... I thought that certain things would be thrown out of the window which in practice haven't been.'

This shift in opinion has been won by the efforts of those who insisted (through their words and practice) that the maintenance of standards of discipline remained a central part of the teacher role. As the headteacher emphasises, the changes in Seaview are about ensuring that pupils assume an active and responsible role in their own learning, assessment and self-discipline. Hence, the process is fundamentally concerned with creating the conditions for a dialogue: a dialogue which presupposes that neither teachers nor pupils will always be correct:

> We are talking about including students on levels of equality in a *dialogue* and no dialogue presupposes that either side must be right as of right. So although, of course, we need to know what students' views are, we are not saying that those views are necessarily right or necessarily acceptable.

Sanctions

As we have noted, one of the headteacher's long-term goals was to improve pupils' sense of self-discipline: by drawing young people actively into the process of assessment and negotiation it is hoped that they will reflect their greater responsibility in improved behaviour and heightened motivation. In trying to express this aim the head originally used the phrase 'the sanction-free school' to describe the kind of institution which he hoped would result. It quickly emerged that this choice of words was probably the very worst move which the headteacher could have made. 'Sanctions' became a major issue in the school and, complicated by some teachers' strength of feeling for/against the changes, for a while it appears that a genuine dilemma went largely unrecognised in the heat of debate.

A small group of teachers undoubtedly used 'the sanctions issue' to further denigrate what they saw as an unworkable approach. For others, however, sanctions presented a genuine area of doubt. As a member of the steering group recalls:

Staff were very uncertain as to what they could and could not do. We'd had hints that, well you shouldn't have detentions because detentions are in themselves negative and perhaps a waste of time. You should be adopting a more positive approach. It was easy to say what we didn't want to do; it was less easy for the staff to be told what they had to do.

In staff meetings, formal in-service events and informal gossip, sanctions became a major concern in the school – the key question was often framed in such a way that there was an apparent clash between, on one hand, the philosophy of pupil participation and negotiation, and on the other, the use of sanctions – the discussion group extract (quoted earlier) is an example of this. In retrospect it is impossible to judge precisely what proportion of staff were genuinely confused about the role of sanctions as opposed to those who used the sanctions issue as a micro-political weapon with which to attack the changes.

Now, four years into the new approaches, the sanctions debate is finally subsiding. The situation has been ameliorated by a number of factors, not least a firm lead from members of the senior management team who, through their personal actions on issues such as lateness and corridor behaviour, have signalled to staff and pupils alike that action will be taken when pupils do not fulfil the school's expectations. The head and his deputies have tried to take a consistent line on sanctions. First, they have argued that the idea of sanctions in itself is compatible with attempts to increase pupil engagement. Second, they have worked with staff to change some sanctions so that they are more in keeping with the school's positive emphasis on achievement.

The following extract is taken from a document relating to a training day which revealed widespread concerns about discipline within the new philosophical framework. In this extract the headteacher makes his position clear: sanctions still exist; it is their nature, use and the assumptions which underlie them which must change. Under the heading, 'Positive Response', the head accepted that the term 'sanction-free' was inappropriate, but argued that 'there seems little point in perpetuating a system of mindless sanctions which are imposed with little regard to any effect they may have or to their relevance to the incident which made them necessary'. He continued:

We should be at pains to discuss pupils' problems in a supportive way in order that they might better come to understand where and how they have gone wrong. If this can be achieved, then the chances of improvement are much greater. YES – pupils *will* still be expected to do 'community service'; pupils *will* be expected to do extra work, or repeat work; pupils *will* have to apologise for rude or inappropriate behaviour; pupils *will* be expected to make up for lost or wasted time; pupils *will* be expected to remain beyond normal school time if it is thought appropriate; pupils *will* be excluded if necessary.

One thing has to be clearly stated: *not everything is negotiable.*

... Action taken must fit the circumstances of the incident and be appropriate to the circumstances of the individual; it must also be seen as a positive attempt to encourage improvement....

There will always be some pupils who do not respond to any regimen, and they will need special consideration. We must, however, beware of subjecting all pupils to a system which is designed to deal with the more recalcitrant among their number. We shall not achieve perfection, but if we treat our pupils in a way which encourages their natural development towards adulthood [and] which gives them a sense of achievement and promotes their sense of self-worth, then we shall succeed in creating a better atmosphere for us all.

The key ideas expressed in this extract are mirrored now in the actions of Seaview staff. In interview, the teachers are keen to emphasise that some traditional sanctions are still used and, like everyone else, they sometimes 'blow their top'; the difference is the context within which their patience is finally exhausted. As a pastoral head of year explains:

> It is a partnership process and [pupils] know when I blow that it is because they haven't fulfilled their half of the bargain. It isn't something like, 'I am in a bad mood today. I'm going to put the whole class in detention'... any kid in my year group knows *why* they are being punished and most of them will openly sit there and say 'Yes, I know. Fair enough.'

Staff, therefore, try to ensure that pupils understand why a particular sanction is being used. In most cases pupils seem to accept the justice of the situation. The importance of this cannot be over-emphasised: research has consistently shown how highly pupils value teachers who are 'fair', and how much they dislike teachers who are arbitrary or biased in their favours (see Gannaway, 1976; Woods, 1983). During our fieldwork we observed a member of senior management as he dealt with a succession of pupils who had in some way conflicted with the school's disciplinary expectations. The seriousness of the incidents ranged from one which the head and deputy agreed required police involvement to relatively minor matters (such as rudeness or name calling) which would soon be forgotten. In all cases, however, the deputy handled the pupils with patience and with concern. He calmly encouraged the pupils to explain their side of the incident and tried to help them see the consequences of their actions for others.

The changes in Seaview have not, however, been limited to recontextualising traditional sanctions. One of the most important changes has involved reworking an old sanction into a more constructive device which maintains the dialogue between teacher and pupil and actively involves the pupils in setting targets for improvement. The Personal Progress Support (PPS) programme is based on a version of the familiar 'report card'. Previously a pupil who was placed on report carried a card which was to be presented to each subject teacher throughout the day and which required a comment on some aspect of the pupil's conduct: similar systems have been criticised for perpetuating the negative labelling of pupils, setting up situations in which they are expected to misbehave or are treated differently, hence encouraging further conflict (Gillborn, 1990, pp. 33–4).

The PPS programme embodies the school's determination to engage pupils in their own learning and assessment in positive ways which stress achievement rather than failure. If pupils have a particular problem they will discuss it with their form tutor and decide upon a particular, achievable goal, such as 'I will arrive on time for lessons' or 'I will not get into arguments during form periods'. They then set themselves a time span (say a week) over which they will monitor their progress. Having recorded their goal and the timescale in the front of the small PPS booklet, the pupils keep a record of their progress, for example, ticking off particular tasks they had to fulfil (recording the date and other relevant details) or keeping a diary of events. If they wish, pupils can ask subject teachers to add their own comments into the record. At the end of the programme the pupils review their achievements with their tutor. As the introductory page of each PPS booklet notes, 'This is a very responsible task you are taking on, and one that can result in a record of real personal achievement'.

The PPS system offers a way of involving pupils in setting their own academic and behavioural agenda. The programme epitomises the wider changes which have taken place in the school – changes which place a premium on the active involvement of the pupils themselves. As a form tutor comments:

> We discussed three targets that he'd have to do; one was getting on with his work quickly, one was to stop talking to friends, the other was to stop walking about. And his first four [comments from teachers] – disaster! Then one out of three [improved]. Now it's about two out of three ...

Although a minority continue to regret the passing of the more traditional (and narrow) teacher role, there is a general feeling that the changes in Seaview are now proving themselves through the actions, achievement and behaviour of the pupils. Of course, there are still disciplinary problems (it would be unrealistic to expect any approach to solve all possible problems), but many teachers told us that the atmosphere of the school and the kinds of issue which arose had both improved significantly. One teacher, whose career in Seaview began well before any moves toward negotiated assessment, describes the improvement:

> There isn't a single class in this school that I feel uncomfortable about going into. In the old days there were lots of classes – if you were on cover, you would look down and you would say, 'My God. I don't want to go in there.' I don't have feelings like that any more. *Ever.*

Conclusions

The changes which have taken place in Seaview have challenged many aspects of school life which were previously taken for granted. The last four years have improved the pupils' experience of school, enhancing their sense of ownership and active engagement. Pupils now play a crucial role in their own assessment and many display a confident sense of their own ability and capacity to improve their performance. The success of the assessment procedures in Seaview, and the pupils' confident use of their RoAs, highlight the need to reconsider the process, as well as the product, of assessment. The integrated and formative nature of assessment in Seaview is crucial; simply 'testing' pupils more often will not achieve the same results. One of the keys to Seaview's success is the supportive, achievement-orientated climate within which the changes have been built. This has meant that even those pupils most likely to be alienated by the threat of academic 'failure' have become more highly motivated and engaged – the following statement is from a teacher in the Special Needs Support department:

> The biggest plus for me is that I have a great struggle getting kids who need literacy help out of the classroom, to be withdrawn for literacy support... [they don't] want to come out for reading help anymore. In the past it was 'Take me out of this lesson; take me out of that lesson; I'll come now'. I don't get that anymore...

It would be wrong, however, to suppose that Seaview has now worked through its problems. Changes in the structure and funding of state education have increased the need for schools to recruit as widely as possible and to counter negative local perceptions which often reflect rumour and gossip rather than fact. This is a crucial issue for Seaview;

public perceptions often lag behind positive changes in schools. Additionally, it should be remembered that some teachers originally misinterpreted the use of dialogue and negotiation in the school, while the local media have yet to demonstrate any better understanding of the issues involved.

The moves towards more active engagement have created new demands on the school. Having improved parental attendance and helped both pupils and parents to feel at ease in discussions with teachers, the school now deals with a client group who are much more willing and able to voice their grievances. The success of the initial changes, therefore, raises new issues and calls for further developments in the school.

Seaview illustrates some of the issues which have arisen in a school which has set out to change the way pupils experience education, to develop a more active role for them in their own assessment and to recognise their potential for improvement. One of the most obvious lessons to emerge is that initial fears about the pupil intake and local community were largely misplaced. When the changes were first mooted many staff were unsure whether pupils and parents could be 'trusted' to take such an active role. The school's success has been built on a rejection of deficit views and a desire to work with the pupils and community. The importance of such a perspective is further explored in the next chapter.

6 Building Shared Respect

The relationship between urban schools and the communities which they serve is often a difficult one. Members of the community may be ambivalent about the usefulness of school (possibly as a result of their own experiences in education), while teachers sometimes come to hold deficit views of the community, blaming parents and pupils for low achievement and poor behaviour in school. In this way a lack of understanding can come to characterise the different views which school and community hold of each other, with neither party appreciating the complex demands acting upon the other nor the variety of goals and values which they may hold. In this context one way forward is to build a solid foundation of greater understanding and mutual respect between school and community.

In settings where there are clear differences between the school and community in terms of social class or ethnic background, it is likely that there will be greater problems of building mutual respect and understanding. This chapter deals with the work of *two* schools; one explores the potential problems raised by social class differences, the other examines issues arising from differences of ethnic background.

The first, Burran School, has already featured in this book (see chapter 4). The central role given to dialogue in Burran reflects a wider belief in the need to build greater understanding, based on mutual respect, as a platform for achievement. The second, Forest School, has experienced significant changes in the ethnic background of its pupil intake. Previously an 'all-white' school, with a long tradition of high academic expectations, the staff are now learning to work with a South Asian community which presents many new challenges and opportunities.

The two schools represent different aspects of the same issue; that is, the need to build strong and active respect between school and community. In the case of Burran, the most pressing need was to build respect for learning within a close-knit working-class community which had no tradition of valuing education. In Forest, the need was to build respect for learners among a school staff who were largely unprepared for the new realities of life in a school serving a predominantly working class South Asian community.

Respect for Learning

> We were very aware that our pupils in this area were underachieving ... we were very conscious that a lot of the problem was we didn't have as close a relationship with families as we should have and that, in other words, the community round here didn't really hold education in high respect, and that on a long-term basis one of the ways of sorting that out is actually to give them respect for education – literally getting through those gates and seeing if there was something in it for them.
>
> *(Deputy headteacher)*

Burran School is located in an area characterised by a large proportion of single-parent families and pensioners living alone. With the closure of the nearby docks in the 1970s the community lost its major source of employment. Consequently there is little economic security, nor much likelihood of improvement in the near future.

Despite the many hardships, the community is stable. Although around one-quarter of the borough's population are of ethnic minority background this figure is not reflected in the school's immediate community, which is predominantly white working class. This reflects both the lack of work and a history of active racism. Parties such as the National Front, for example, have a comparatively good electoral track record here.

The school serves a 'strong' community in the sense of its existing homogeneity and culture (Carspecken, 1991, p. 8). It can be difficult to forge genuine links with such a community; the existing boundaries can effectively exclude outsiders who – although perhaps with the best intentions – struggle to be accepted by a community with a deep mistrust of authority. In such cases schools and teachers can be seen as at best irrelevant, and at worst a potential source of trouble for the community itself.

90

In trying to build greater respect for learning amongst the community, several staff in Burran realised that education would have to prove its worth in terms of the reality of life for the community itself: teachers and education had to become respect-worthy in the eyes of the community. In the early 1980s this view crystallised in the school's bid to the LEA for enhanced resourcing as a 'community' school. As one of the architects of the bid reflects:

> It will take a long time but eventually we will be able to help anybody in the community and this centre will actually *mean* something in their lives. So when their children come or their nieces or nephews or whatever, they would actually, if you like, be pushing the child in the same direction as we were, saying, 'Yes, education is important. Yes, we are going to go and help you. Yes, we think we should be involved'. That was really the main aim of going community.

The decision to 'go community', as this teacher puts it, marked a critical turning point in the school's development. As the current headteacher (in post for eighteen months) observes, 'a lot of staff argue that the improvements that have been made in the school are basically derived from a completely different approach which took place when we became a community school'.

The 'completely different approach' involves a commitment actively to involve the community in education, whether as parents, governors, community representatives on school committees or as students attending occasional classes or taught courses which lead to external examinations. By bringing the community into the school, and by using outreach activities to take the school into the community, Burran is building respect for learning by demonstrating its effectiveness as an important part of the life of the community.

Education and Community Involvement

Many of the advances which the school has made rely on changing perspectives and practices amongst the teaching staff. It is also the case, however, that increased funding (as part of the school's change to 'community' status) acted as a major impetus to new developments. In physical terms the school's community function is reflected in the various buildings which make up the Burran site. The 11–18 school is part of a complex of buildings – a confusion of contrasting design styles – which have built up around a central recreation area. These include a small theatre, a gymnasium, a further education block, a youth centre, creche and community lounge (a multi-purpose area comprising a cafe area and large hall). The latter serves a variety of purposes, and, like most of the site, is available for community use throughout the week. These facilities are an important resource for the community and for pupils. We were told by pupils, for example, that the youth club offers somewhere for them to meet socially without the fear of 'invasion' or violence by gangs from other schools or localities.

Adult education in Burran is not limited to the further education block. The school has an 'open door' policy which extends to mainstream classes. Adults who wish to follow a particular course may negotiate access to any upper school lesson (as well as to the sixth form). In addition, adult education classes are timetabled throughout the day so that, for example, a group of school children might be working in a room next to 'community students' (ranging from retired people through to some who have only recently left compulsory schooling). Community students often work towards external certification – hoping to improve their position in the job market – but many simply attend to expand an existing interest or to pursue a hobby. Adults and school pupils, therefore, routinely mingle in Burran – in the corridor, around the site, in coffee areas and sometimes in classrooms. Unlike some 'community schools', it is not the case that the site is dominated by school pupils during the day and then taken over by community students at night.

Less than a decade ago Burran was a very different school. When the idea of becoming a community school was first raised, many staff were fearful of a flood of 'unknown' adults entering the site. These understandable fears were addressed during a series of staff meetings before the changes were introduced. The results, however, have been more positive than most dared to imagine. Carefully worked-out procedures have been developed so that, for example, staff courteously enquire where adults wish to be and offer to guide them there, taking them to a member of senior staff if there is any doubt about the legitimacy of their purpose. Staff view the adoption of such procedures as the reason why there have been very few disturbing incidents as a result of community access to the site.

The variety of school users has, in fact, worked to improve the atmosphere of the school. A senior teacher explains:

> One of the fears of many of the staff was having children running around, going to creche, and having adults in the school and not knowing who they were ... But that has been a bonus because the rest of the school have had to see these children walk down the corridor and they respect them, like they respect the older people ... Adults that come in for classes, they are really impressed with the way the children behave. People think, a secondary school in [the inner city], the kids will be charging down the corridors. But our kids realise that there will be little babies and there will be old grannies or whatever going down the corridor and they respect the fact that they are part of the school.

The benefits of the changes go much further than an improvement in corridor behaviour. In the following sections we examine the most important changes and their consequences.

Building Effective Participation

> I get very irritated when [schools] say, 'We have been doing community education for years'. But when you get down to it with a lot of them... what they actually mean is they have had a parents' room where they have stuck parents – not involved them in the school – and given them a cup of coffee. Now that is not what I call community ed. or effective participation.
>
> *(Senior teacher: Community)*

Burran expresses its aims through a broad commitment to serve the needs of, and be accountable to, the community. When we invited staff, parents, pupils and adult students to talk about the school in detail a range of different concerns emerged. At the level of specific initiatives it is clear that certain groups benefit directly while others enjoy a less immediate dividend. At a whole-school level, however, the various initiatives add up to a different culture of schooling from which all groups within the school draw some benefit.

As members of the community with a vested interest in the school, parents represent a potential source of support of which many schools fail to take advantage. Burran operates an explicit policy of parental involvement which means that whenever a disciplinary problem arises they are quick to contact the pupils' home. Not all families are supportive, or even sympathetic, but experience has shown that even within such a disadvantaged area active opposition to the school is comparatively rare. Nevertheless, contacting home requires sensitivity and a member of senior management is usually consulted before teachers make any move to take 'problems' to parents' doorsteps. A deputy headteacher explains:

> You have got to be very careful. If we know it is a family that is difficult and anti-school – which there are – we have to come about it in another way or we have to tread carefully... So we have got to be careful with *some* individuals but *generally* it works very well... I think what we are very good at here is getting, straight away, contact with parents. You know, phoning, calling round in the evenings. We have got staff who are home-liaison teachers... We use them to go home that evening, to say to the parents, 'This is the sort of problem we have had today, we really need to get to grips with this'.

Where parents attend classes as adult students there is, of course, a direct bearing upon home–school relationships. Parents who had attended classes during the school day, or in the evening, listed several ways in which their views of the school had changed. One of the most immediate effects was an increased personal respect for teachers as professionals doing a highly demanding job. In addition, several parents told us that they were now much more confident in their dealings with teachers and their readiness to approach the school about things which bothered them. This reflects both a personal sense of growth through education and, more immediately, the realisation that (whatever the school used to be like) it is now a welcoming and understanding place:

DIMENSIONS OF DISCIPLINE

[When I was here as a pupil] the front door you could only use if you were a fifth year or a prefect. And to come back in it as a community school – it did me good because then you can relate better when your children are here. Because I had this fixed idea – it is like everything else – this is the authority [up here: high hand gesture] and this is you [lowly gesture], we are not on a level. But now it is more of an equal, you know.

(Parent / adult student)

I find with the teachers, if you have got a problem and you phone up, there is always someone to see you. You can bring your child along and try and sort it out. There is a kind of spirit in the school where you feel welcome. When you go to some schools to see the headteacher, you have got to *'Sit here'* and *'Wait'*, you know.

(Parent / adult student)

The school's work with the community includes links with outreach centres located outside the immediate school site. Such work has practical benefits for those who do not live near the school, but equally important is the symbolic value of moving outside the school walls and physically entering the community. A local resident, who has been particularly active in the recently formed Tenants' Association, emphasises the importance of matching action to rhetoric: 'They could run the club from *here* [the main school building] but they go *into* the community... You get a lot of this lip service of Equal Opps but seeing it in practice is a different thing.'

In addition, the school has helped with the formation of a support group for new members of the community who have fled persecution in their home countries. By offering a base for a refugee self-help group the school is now continuing the practical support which it was initially able to offer through taught language courses. Such work has an important effect on the life of the school, especially where it demonstrates the strength and resourcefulness of groups which traditionally suffer marginal or even 'outsider' status within the white working-class culture of the community:

We have quite a few people in wheelchairs, we have some mentally handicapped people, we have Asian women's groups... all these things – without stating it – just the fact that they are around, and they are being accepted by us and the children accept it, is a very positive move. But they don't always accept them out in the community, so that is a positive step.

(Deputy headteacher)

In this way the school's acceptance of traditionally marginalised and excluded groups can begin to react back onto the community. Long-standing prejudices and deep-seated racism cannot be changed over night. Neither can one institution, such as a school, bring about wholesale change in practices and beliefs which have a long history and which draw support from so many different sources within society. Nevertheless, the pupils' behaviour in and around the school does at least offer some hope of improvement in the community. Additionally, there are many ways in which moves to encourage the active participation of the community are having a real impact on the day-to-day experience of schooling inside Burran. Once again, the benefits are spread across both the community and the school itself.

Adult Students and School Pupils

When you are mature you give as much as you take away.

(Adult student)

Burran's improving local reputation is making it easier for adults to take the difficult step of walking through the school gates for the first time. Some adult students find the move easier than others. The school holds fewer fears for those who left compulsory schooling within the recent past and several teachers mentioned to us that pupils who had rejected the school at sixteen returned a few years later keen to continue their studies. For older adults, especially those with children who have been out of education for some time, the decision to return to school (any school) can be fraught with uncertainty and fear of ridicule or embar-rassment:

DIMENSIONS OF DISCIPLINE

When I wanted to come in as an adult student the first thing [my husband] said to me was, 'People won't want you in the classroom amongst children' and 'they are going to laugh at you'. That put me off at first, but then the next year I was determined: 'Regardless of whether they laugh at me or not I am going to go'. And I did come and I found the situation was completely different. I enjoyed it. I gained from them and they gained from me. And it has built my confidence up because I had lost that confidence... It was three years I stayed here and I enjoyed every minute, I am still coming back and still phoning up, I enjoyed it so much.

(Adult student)

Adult students can gain both enjoyment and personal satisfaction from their studies. Some work towards specific qualifications which, coupled with the confidence they gain from success, can open up new employment prospects. For others there is no realistic chance of employment, perhaps because of their age or family commitments, but their time at Burran is nevertheless a valued part of their life. Indeed, many adult students attend classes purely for the intrinsic reward of learning new skills or meeting new people; there is no obligation to study towards a formal examination. This kind of enthusiasm can set an important example to the school pupils who see local people willingly attending the school, keen to take advantage of opportunities already open to the youth.

Similarly, the work of adult students can help to challenge a range of assumptions. During our work in Burran, for example, we were told of cases where non-academic subjects, which pupils sometimes disregard as worthless, gained greater status because pupils saw adults coming into the school purely to enjoy the work for its own sake. Similarly, the gendered nature of certain subjects can be questioned where pupils see adults at work in areas which contradict popular stereotypes – for example, men studying keyboard and typographical skills under the direction of a woman.

Where adult students and school pupils are both working towards examinations the shared demands of school work can lead to mutually supportive relationships, each learning from the example of the other, each acting as a source of encouragement and strength:

> I remember the last exam I took with Jackie [school pupil]. Because after the exam she said to me, 'What did you think of it? I do hope that you pass, even if I fail. I hope that *you* pass'. And I was saying to myself, 'Oh I do wish that she would pass'. Because she needed it, she was young and she needed that extra – I didn't care if I failed, I just wanted her to pass. And she had the same [feelings].

(Adult student)

Effective Participation and Respect for Learning

The Burran School has come a long way but has further to go. It is still the case, for example, that only a minority of parents attend the annual meeting to discuss the governors' report. Similarly, most active community representatives are drawn from a particular age range, with 16–30 year olds rarely being involved. Burran is making genuine progress but nevertheless faces an uphill struggle, not least as a result of changing policy and funding arrangements which threaten some of the school's current community operations. The LEA is moving 16–18 provision into separate sixth-form colleges and, although adult education will remain on the school site, the loss of the sixth form will damage the continuity of community provision which the school presently offers. Despite these problems, Burran stands as a clear example of what can be achieved when a school sets out to build effective community participation in learning.

The decision to enhance the school's work with the community was not explicitly related to discipline, yet many of the initiatives have had a direct impact on pupils' motivation and work within the school. The pupils have begun to share something of the adults' enthusiasm for education, they have questioned traditional expectations and gained in responsibility through the shared use of a busy school site. The school's reputation has improved and there are signs of genuine progress; rolls are improving, as is parental attendance and support for the school.

Through its work, therefore, the Burran School sets a strong example, demonstrating the power of learning in a community which has no tradition of valuing education. In other urban contexts community respect for learning may already be strong – in some cases, however, there is a need to build greater respect for learners among teachers.

Respect for Learners

Our second account of school–community relationships focuses on a school which has a predominantly South Asian pupil intake. Some of the issues which emerge touch on existing debates about education in a multi-ethnic society and it may be helpful to begin by clarifying our understanding of certain key terms.

In the field of 'race' and education 'respect' is sometimes seen as a soft term, lacking the hard edge required of any serious attempt to challenge racism in society. In outlining the main differences between the language of multiculturalism and anti-racism, for example, Brandt (1986, p. 121) contrasts the former's concern with 'culture' ('awareness, equality, parity of esteem') with the latter's focus on 'racism' ('equal human rights, power, justice'). Within Brandt's analysis the former is presented as a tool of the establishment whilst the latter is seen as promising real change. In fact, the distinction is a difficult one to maintain in practice. Whilst respect certainly includes 'parity of esteem' the practice of respect, as this account suggests, has very real consequences for equality of human rights, power and justice.

Building understanding between schools and their communities can be especially difficult where there are differences of tradition, religion and language which reflect the pupils' ethnic background. This account looks at a school which, as it attempts to build a better understanding of its pupil population, may serve as a critical case, illuminating issues and approaches which have a wider significance. Relatively little school-based research has examined education in settings where South Asian pupils are in the majority. Existing work suggests that in such cases teachers are likely to hold strong stereotypes of South Asian communities (e.g. as rigidly structured and patriarchal) and to see them as responsible for limiting pupils' opportunities (see Gillborn, 1992; Shepherd, 1987).

Forest School

A school with a long and distinguished history of academic achievement, during the 1970s and 1980s Forest attracted an increasing number of Asian pupils, principally from families of Pakistani origin who are Punjabi/Urdu speakers and members of the Muslim faith. The changing character of migration from the Indian subcontinent, and the poor conditions in the inner-city area where they settled, had direct consequences for Forest School. The school's headteacher (appointed in the late 1980s) describes that point in Forest's history as follows:

> By the early '80s the school's population was getting to the point where there was 60 to 70 per cent ethnic minority students and the really interesting shift was that it was a different kind of youngster that was coming in. These were families who had not necessarily come from areas of any kind of affluence; families who didn't have experience of formal schooling before coming here; families who had been in rural, very poor areas of Northern Pakistan living in fairly poor and inadequate and overcrowded housing within the city centre. And the youngsters coming here started to bring with them considerable disadvantage.

Whilst the proportion of Asian pupils continued to increase, there was a decrease in the number of white pupils entering the school – a phenomenon which some teachers now refer to as the 'white flight'. A teacher who has worked in Forest for over twenty years recalls how, in the eyes of long-established staff, the ethnic composition seemed to change quickly: 'This school grew rapidly from a fifty-fifty mix to 70 or 80 per cent Asian, 20 per cent white. And once it got to that stage it rapidly went to over 90 per cent. I think that was a conscious decision by the white community to opt away from the school.'

With the changing composition of the pupil population, the teaching staff at Forest faced an enormous challenge. The school has a long-established, traditionalist history with a stable staff. The headteacher has no illusions about the size of the task facing the school:

> I came to a school that was very low on morale. I have never come to a school that was so low ... A staff who were utterly bewildered by

what they had seen happen and couldn't understand why it had happened... there was a sense here of frustration, a sense amongst the staff that they had been de-skilled ... At my very first staff meeting here one of the staff said to me, 'The trouble with this school is we have got the wrong children here'. And that was the pervading feeling.

Respect with Equal Value

Finding 'the middle path' is how the headteacher describes the current management style which has been adopted in order to help move the school forward: that is, trying to work with the staff, using small groups of committed teachers as a spur to encourage development among their colleagues. The head is wary of too much direct confrontation and sensitive to local 'racial' politics and the pitfalls of seeming to label white people as racist by definition – what the Burnage enquiry termed 'symbolic' or 'moral' anti-racism (Macdonald *et al*, 1989, pp. 347–8). In particular, the head is critical of approaches which do not venture beyond a basic acknowledgement of the variety of traditions and beliefs which exist in a multicultural society. The key to progress, the head argues, is respect for all pupils and their communities:

> You have got to want to learn and you have got to want to put an equal value upon the things you are learning... You haven't got to put them in a hierarchy ... the whole problem of 'multiculturalism' is that it assumes that provided you know how *'these people'* live all will be well. What it often ends up with is people being stacked with knowledge about how *'these people'* live and in parenthesis, but unsaid, 'And isn't it quaint'. And 'this is not the way we do it' and 'the way we do it is better'.

Hence, the headteacher rejects celebratory versions of multiculturalism which give primacy to images of 'strange' or exotic cultures without challenging existing racial stereotypes. In contrast, the head emphasises respect for people and the things they value. As a consequence of this position, there are certain issues which there can be no compromise on – and where the 'middle path' cannot be taken. One such issue concerns the status accorded to pupils' mother-tongue:

When I came here the kids weren't *allowed* to use their first language. That was one of the policies that I said we were not having; 'it is the children's first language and they will use it'.

(Headteacher)

Language is more than a mere system of communication; it also fulfils a powerful affective role, forging a bond between members of the same linguistic community and excluding all others. The headteacher decided that the aim of respect with equal value could not condone a rule which, within the school, clearly defined the Asian pupils' first language as at best inappropriate, at worst inferior. For this reason the head decided to abandon the rule against the use of community languages in school.

However, there was some feeling among the staff that pupils were using their bilingualism as a means of excluding teachers from certain conversations:

A teacher will say to a kid, 'Shafeeq, will you get on with that work' and Shafeeq will look to his mate and say something in Punjabi. They will both go into fits of giggles. The teacher feels undermined: [teacher] 'What did you say?' [pupil] 'Nothing'.

The headteacher recognised that, on occasion, the Asian pupils were clearly using their first language in this way and was aware of the very serious teacher–pupil conflicts which might arise as a result (see Gillborn, 1990; Mac an Ghaill, 1988; Wright, 1985). Rather than resorting to the previous ban, however, staff were encouraged to look beyond the language issue and to see the problem as a manifestation of a more fundamental conflict – reflecting the distance between the white teachers and the Asian pupils. In the following sections we examine some of the ways in which the school has begun to close this gap, according their pupils and feeder communities genuine respect with equal value.

Effective Communication

When discussing the ways in which the school has changed in recent years the headteacher begins by emphasising the centrality of the community liaison officer: 'We couldn't exist without him'.

Not everything boils down to money: much of the school's progress rests on staff's insight, imagination and determination to work with the community for the benefit of the school and pupils. Without the funding to support a full-time community liaison officer, however, a vital and dynamic link between the school and the South Asian community would be lost. As the head explains:

> All the parents know now that they can ring the school and they only have to ask for him; they get put through to somebody who is Punjabi speaking. That has been really important. [He] speaks all the dialects of Punjabi that we need ... We *must* have somebody here who can take telephone calls, who can meet and greet parents. What happens is parents all know now, the word has got round that he is here and parents will now freely come in. We have no problem with parents coming into school, *none whatsoever*.

Sending newsletters and reports home in community languages is a basic first step which, according to the Elton Report, all multiracial schools should follow (DES, 1989, para. 154). In isolation, however, this can amount to little more than a cosmetic exercise. Even if parents are literate in one of the community languages which are used, the communication is merely one-way: school to home. Schools must find ways of giving parents a voice. In Forest School the community liaison officer is building a positive and genuine dialogue between school and community by fulfilling just such a role. He enables parents effectively to communicate with the school; he is approachable, understands their concerns and can help them to strike up a dialogue with any teacher or group within the school.

The community liaison officer describes his role in simple but far-reaching terms: 'to bridge the gap between school and homes, and to make the school a community school'. He joined the staff at Forest in the late 1980s and has made an important contribution to the developing relationship between school and community. On a daily basis the community liaison officer fulfils a vital linking function, offering an immediate voice to parents with whom the majority of staff are unable to converse. Yet his importance goes beyond communication: he is a respected member of both the school and its South Asian feeder community – he understands the expectations and pressures which act upon both parties.

The success of the community liaison officer at Forest illustrates the crucial importance of giving black perspectives a central role in the operation of schools. This is not to say that black teachers, for example, are automatically expert in multicultural/anti-racist education nor should they be limited to any particular aspect of schools' curricular or pastoral operations (Ranger, 1988). The point at issue here goes beyond the need simply to employ more black teachers; it involves the need to listen to, respect and respond constructively to the views and concerns of black communities.

Putting Principles into Practice

A report on a racist murder and racial harassment in Manchester (Macdonald *et al*, 1989) highlighted the importance of actively involving the white community in discussions of ethnicity and anti-racist initiatives in education. Forest tries to act in ways which embody its commitment to serve several communities; it is concerned not to replace the exclusion of one ethnic group with the exclusion of another. Whenever a high proportion of Asian students is likely to be absent for a religious festival the school ensures that special activities are timetabled for the white pupils. In this way Forest seeks to demonstrate its active respect for *all* the communities which it serves. In a school such as this, where the large majority of pupils are of South Asian origin, it might be supposed that white pupils would feel isolated or of secondary importance; by consciously working to demonstrate its respect for every group within its pupil population, the school is acknowledging and valuing ethnic diversity without causing resentment or misunderstanding.

A series of events surrounding the Gulf conflict of 1990/91 highlights the ways in which the school has tried to act according to its principles of respect with equal value for ethnic groups.

In the latter part of 1990, as coalition forces prepared for what was to become the Gulf War, political tensions in the Middle East had direct consequences for life in the United Kingdom. As tensions rose a popular assumption seemed to be that all Asians were Muslims and necessarily supported Saddam Hussein (Khanum, 1991). The assumption was insupportable but, as hostilities began, the implication that Asian people represented a 'fifth column' undoubtedly gained some popular support. On occasion the tensions found expression in violence: several areas reported vandalised mosques and increased attacks on Asian people, including racial harassment in schools (Runnymede Trust, 1991, pp. 9–10).

Clearly Forest School was in an extremely difficult position. The majority of its pupils belonged to an ethnic group which was already subject to increased harassment as a result of a war against a regime which made public appeals to its Islamic background. This took place at a time when the assertiveness of Muslim communities in Britain was reaching a new peak, especially among the youth (Modood, 1990a and b). Some white pupils had close relatives involved in military action in the Gulf. A majority of its Asian pupils were not only excited by current events (wanting to talk about the conflict and discuss the latest news); they were also clear about the fact that they did not automatically accept the political analysis which was offered in the news media. The headteacher recalls the atmosphere which developed in the build-up towards war:

> The children were very clear. They wanted to talk about Saddam Hussein. The blackboards were covered with 'Victory to Saddam' and we had leaflets from outside being left all round the place, about Saddam Hussein. And we were in close contact with the police because the police were very concerned that we were going to get targeted for NF [National Front] activity...

The school clearly faced a potentially explosive situation and the gravity of the issues drew the staff together in a very constructive way:

> During October/November [as the armed build-up continued] one of the really positive things was that as a staff we discussed how we were going to handle it – when we saw the crisis emerging – and we decided that we were going to be *utterly* neutral about it but allow children to talk about it as and when they wanted.

All staff were asked to monitor the situation and report to the senior management any statements which pupils made about the conflict. In turn, a member of the senior team would speak to the pupil concerned, attempting to reinforce the sensitivity of the situation while maintaining the school's refusal to take sides and the right of pupils to their own views:

> We've a handful of white kids here some of whom have got brothers in the Forces. Where a kid in class said, 'I hope all the English and the Americans are bombed to bits', I saw the kid and said, 'Look, you are entitled to your views about Saddam Hussein but you have got to remember that other people have other views'...

Similarly white pupils were encouraged to respect the right of their Asian peers to hold opposing views. Additionally, support was offered for those pupils who felt vulnerable to attack: 'a number of kids were desperately scared because they thought they were going to be targeted for white aggression'.

Initially the school's handling of the tensions surrounding the Gulf War proceeded more smoothly than anyone had dared to expect: at one point it seemed like 'a bit of damp squib' to one teacher, who recalls that although some of the pupils were very concerned with events in the Gulf, 'They tended to keep it away from us [the teachers]'. However, this relative calm was broken by an incident, outside school hours, which involved pupils from several local schools. An attack was organised against a mainly white school in the city – a 'raid' which included physical assaults – and in which pupils from Forest figured prominently: one estimate is that close to one hundred pupils from the school were involved.

An incident of such severity presented a serious challenge to the school's attempts to build mutual respect and understanding. The school's response was to arrange for each year group to be addressed by key members of the black community as well as by police and senior teachers in the school. The pupils responsible for the raid were asked to identify themselves to the school, with a clear explanation about the circumstances under which they might face prosecution. The head admits that the appeal could have fallen on deaf ears and, under different circumstances, the strategy might have failed. However, the school's response – and its ultimate success – has to be seen within the wider context of a commitment to respect with equal value, and its recent record of putting that principle into practice. The result surprised everyone:

DIMENSIONS OF DISCIPLINE

We had them queueing down the corridor. Now that is unprece-
dented because the police normally get no co-operation at all. None.
They came in, one by one, 'I want to tell you my part'. One after the
other, 'We didn't think.' 'We never realised.'

The incident and its resolution powerfully demonstrate what can
be achieved when a school pursues a commitment to respect with equal
value. Although the incident itself has many unique features, there are
broad lessons to be learned from the school's handling of the tensions
surrounding the Gulf War.

The first lesson concerns the value of whole-school planning
which aimed at sensitive and consistent dealings with pupils. The
school's position was clearly communicated to pupils in arenas which
included year assemblies, form groups and one-to-one conversations.
The adoption of a school-wide approach to issues arising from the Gulf
War, one which emphasised the right of pupils to hold different views,
was an important breakthrough. Crucially, this approach included monitoring and referral procedures which helped to support staff and maintain consistency of practice in their dealings with pupils.

Second, the school's experience highlights the contribution of the
black community itself: the school's response signals its readiness to hear
the voice of the community whilst simultaneously demonstrating an
awareness of the realities of life in a society which is both multiracial and
multi-racist (Cohen and Bains, 1988). The school engaged with the situation, presenting a consistent line (backed by both black community lead-
ers and the police) which offered a way through the crisis.

Conclusions

In this chapter we have focused on two schools which illustrate particular aspects of the same issue: the need to build mutual respect between
school and community.

Teachers in Burran have started to rebuild the community's
respect for learning by way of a series of initiatives which actively involve
the community in education. The school has benefitted in many ways; its

local reputation has improved, rolls are up and a changed atmosphere has resulted from the school's commitment to the local community.

In Forest School staff are beginning to move away from the deficit model which once characterised their view of the South Asian community from which most of their pupils are drawn. Progress has been slow and painful but there are signs of fundamental changes as the principles of respect with equal value are enacted on a school-wide basis. Although neither school would claim to have solved its problems, both are making genuine progress within a context of struggle. They epitomise the achievements which can be made when urban communities are viewed as potential partners in the learning process rather than as a source of problems.

7 Developing New Perspectives

In this book we have presented accounts of five urban secondary schools located in areas of considerable socio-economic disadvantage in the South, Midlands and North of England. All the schools were concerned about motivation and achievement and, more generally, about the 'currency' of education in settings where mobility tends to be low and unemployment is high. The schools were chosen because they had all acknowledged the need for change and all seemed to be making progress in difficult contexts.

The study, which was carried out in 1990–1991, was supported by the DES and builds on the work of the Committee of Enquiry into Discipline which was chaired by Lord Elton (1988–1989). Data were mainly gathered through interviews with teachers, pupils and, in some cases, parents. Each account has been discussed with members of the school concerned.

The Elton Report suggested that, whatever their particular social context, schools can bring about improvement. In a section headed 'Schools make a Difference', the Committee wrote:

> The message to heads and teachers is clear. It is that they have the power, through their own efforts, to improve standards of work and behaviour and the life chances of their pupils.

(Elton Report, 1989, p. 88)

The Committee's recommendations have been widely welcomed and moves have been made to ensure their implementation, but there was some concern that the Committee's terms of reference might have led to 'an unwarranted separation of pupil behaviour from their academic development' (Hargreaves, 1989, p. 2). A similar concern was expressed by Galloway *et al* (1989, p. 102) who argued that research

109

should give more attention to the links between discipline and pupil motivation. These observations are echoed by Jones (1989, p. 264):

> There is still an emphasis on the management of misbehaviour in schools being dealt with as a phenomenon isolated from the wider context of the ethos and organisation of the school.

In the research reported here we have tried to address these concerns.

How Schools are Rethinking Discipline

In the schools we worked with discipline is not narrowly conceived as the imposition of rules by those in authority but is acknowledged to be an enabling and integrating principle: discipline is what links institutional purposefulness and orderliness with individual purposefulness and orderliness. The linkage is effected, in practical terms, through the school's concentration on various features which we have called the *dimensions of discipline*: expectations, consistency, dialogue, engagement and respect.

What the five dimensions have in common is a capacity for redefining relationships in terms of a certain quality of reciprocity. *Dialogue* is perhaps the most obvious and concrete example of the way in which teachers and pupils are brought into a different relationship with one another. In a similar way, *respect* rests on mutuality of esteem between teachers and pupils and between the school and the community; *expectations* and *engagement* are about mutuality of confidence and commitment; *consistency* is manifest in the frameworks of common agreement which hold the behaviours of both teachers and pupils to account.

The five schools were all rethinking discipline as a means of reconciling concerns about individual and social conduct with concerns about learning and achievement. Each school, depending on how it was dealing with its past, analysing its present and planning for its future, has prioritised a different dimension, while recognising the importance and inter-relatedness of the other dimensions.

110   DIMENSIONS OF DISCIPLINE

Two accounts (Milner School and Reid School) focus on overall organisational frameworks and the need to build common understanding within the team of teachers; two accounts (Burran School and Seaview School) focus on ways of helping pupils to exercise their right to learn and to value and understand their own progress; the final account looks at the relationship between schools and their communities.

In Milner School (chapter 2) teachers are directly concerned with the issue of expectations. They are coming to see that an emphasis on achievement is not at odds with the spirit of a caring school but, indeed, is essential if disadvantaged pupils are to have an opportunity to change traditional post-school destinations and life chances. An over-riding concern is to rebuild motivation by helping young people have some sense of a future that is worth striving for.

In Reid School (chapter 3) the concern is to build strong, supportive links among teachers and to work to an agreed statement of values. A strategy has been developed for helping members of staff play an active role in the formulation and implementation of whole-school policy. Despite personal differences in outlook among individual members of the school staff, it has proved possible to build professional commitment that is manifest to pupils in consistency of practice.

In the Burran School (chapter 4) dialogue is used as a way of building shared understanding between teachers and parents and between teachers and pupils. The school is ready to listen and to adapt. The new frameworks that guide personal and inter-personal behaviour are firm and clear and they apply, with a due sense of fairness, to teachers as well as to pupils. Disruptive behaviours are handled sensitively rather than punitively; what the school means by 'appropriate behaviour' is explained and explored in ways that prevent pupils and parents from experiencing the school's code of conduct as a bureaucratic imposition that is designed solely to control.

In Seaview School (chapter 5) the development of new assessment procedures is proving an effective strategy for increasing pupils' active engagement in their own learning and providing them with a clearer sense of individual progress. The account also shows how long it took for the majority of teachers to feel at ease with the changes. For many, giving pupils a voice in their own schooling was a fundamental challenge to strongly held assumptions, but, after a difficult period of review and adjustment, real progress is being made.

The final account (chapter 6) suggests how important it is for schools to demonstrate understanding and respect for the community, and for the community to demonstrate its respect and support for what the school is trying to do. For example, one school is developing a range of opportunities for greater participation by parents and members of the community, and pupils are able to see how educational courses and qualifications are valuable to, and valued by, adults. In another school we see how teachers, in the face of a highly sensitive and potentially inflammatory situation, were able to sustain and exemplify their regard for learners and what they bring, from different cultures, to enrich the task of learning.

Developing New Perspectives

Each of the five schools we worked with was thinking, collectively, about the nature and purpose of discipline. They were not just schools that were changing but schools that were trying to understand how and why they were changing and how and why society is changing around them. Looking across the experience of the five schools we can identify two areas in which perspectives were changing most radically: perspectives on discipline in the context of whole-school organisational development and perspectives on discipline in the context of pupils and their learning.

Discipline in the Context of Whole-School Organisational Development

All the schools were involved with change at the whole-school level. It is important to highlight this since discipline has often, in the past, been seen as a reliably stable and contained area of school life. The accounts presented in the earlier chapters suggest that discipline, far from being a self-contained system, affects many aspects of schooling: rethinking discipline means rethinking a range of inter-related aspects of school life.

112

In particular, each school acknowledges the importance of shared understanding. Traditional responses to 'the discipline problem' have tended to focus on the figure of the lone (usually male) disciplinarian, invariably located within the ranks of middle to senior management. The schools whose work we document emphasise collegiality and coherence – not only at the level of policy and practice, but also at the level of values.

Moreover, all the schools were sharply aware of the difficulty of sustaining a mutually supportive climate during the uncertainties and upheavals of change – particularly change which involves rethinking the structure and meaning of discipline. Whenever the institutional *status quo* is challenged there are likely to be some teachers who will view themselves as losers in the new order. The danger then is that the staff body may fracture around different interest groups. Situations of this sort are not only stressful for teachers but may also lead to worsening disciplinary problems as pupils perceive, and possibly take advantage of, inconsistency in the attitudes and actions of their teachers. What matters, at a time of change, is whether the leadership of the school can maintain a sense of commitment within the staff as a whole.

It is also important for heads and senior staff in schools to recognise that schools do not develop at a uniform rate and that progress within any school is bound to have its own idiosyncratic ups and downs. What matters, in the face of setbacks, is that a school maintains its underlying philosophy and sense of overall purpose.

Our accounts illustrate that change is a highly complex process and that many of the most important outcomes only emerge slowly. To date, the schools we worked with show many signs of improvement. These include enhanced pupil motivation, better parental and community participation in school life, and more positive teacher–pupil interactions in the classroom and around the school. These improvements represent some of the most important outcomes of the changes that are taking place in perspective and practice. Rethinking the ways in which schools can raise expectations and discharge their general responsibility for ensuring that pupils learn is a difficult task. Progress must be judged against a realistic time scale. Schools have to understand the need for sustained optimism and for a continued investment of effort if progress is to be maintained.

Discipline in the Context of Pupils and Their Learning

All our schools were, at some level, recreating a sense of purposefulness and orderliness *through* a reconceptualisation of discipline. In our view, no school is likely to be successful in such an undertaking unless it is prepared to change its perspective on pupils and what they are capable of achieving.

As we noted in chapter 1, each of the five schools is located in an area where average levels of disadvantage are significantly higher than is the norm for England and Wales. This is an important fact of which the schools are rightly aware: lack of adequate food, clothing or shelter present real obstacles to learning. But although disadvantage may manifest itself in behavioural disturbance and non-attendance, it should not be assumed that it will necessarily do so. Nor should it be assumed that children who experience disadvantage cannot succeed academically. As Wehlage *et al* have observed, 'Students do not fail simply because they are black or poor or pregnant or from a single parent home. They fail, in part, because schools are not responsive to the conditions and problems accompanying these personal and socio-economic characteristics' (1989, pp. 50–51). Raising expectations is not a substitute for support but a way of ensuring that the support offered by schools is enabling.

There was, among our schools, an overriding concern to lift individual and collective aspiration through building a sense of self-worth. It has been said that, for many young people, schooling is an experience that threatens their confidence on a daily basis (Oakes and Lipton, 1990, p. 62). We did not see this: instead, the schools set out to build or restore confidence, and to make every effort to sustain it. Academic demands are not muted in these schools, but at the same time pupils are not threatened or overwhelmed by them. To be successful at school, children must believe that they are capable and they must be helped to act on that belief.

It is clear that the schools are increasingly concerned to encourage a more active role for pupils in the management and monitoring of their own learning. Giving pupils more responsibility does not mean that teachers are abdicating responsibility. Rather, it enables pupils to understand what constitutes academic progress (for instance, seeing how they have improved and how they can set goals for the future), and to appreciate the ways in which their actions can affect the wellbeing and capacity to learn of their peers. Such changes rest on a heightening of respect for pupils by teachers, and a heightening of respect among parents for education and for their children as learners.

Summary

In conclusion, we draw together our observations across the five schools in a form that might be used as a basis for school review and in-service activity.

1. Narrow conceptions of discipline which emphasise the centrality of control and punishment are giving way to broader conceptions which emphasise the positive ways in which discipline influences and relates to individual and collective achievement.

2. Within this broader conceptualisation, discipline has certain key – and inter-related – dimensions:

- Expectations
- Consistency

These dimensions relate primarily to the ways in which teachers work together to construct and sustain frameworks that guide conduct and learning.

- Dialogue
- Engagement

These dimensions relate primarily to the ways in which teachers are seeking to motivate and build different relationships with their pupils.

- Respect

This dimension relates to the positive regard felt by different partners – teachers, pupils, parents and other members of the community – for themselves and for each other.

3. Translating these dimensions into practical terms, we would look for evidence of progress under two headings: *new perspectives on whole-school organisation; new perspectives on pupils' capacity for learning.*

4. Evidence of progress in relation to *whole-school organisation* would include the following:

   • The staff are collectively moving towards a coherent and agreed set of values which are reliably acted on by all staff and operate in relation to all aspects of school life. In short, the school has a sense of itself.

   • The school is populated by people, both teachers and pupils, who are becoming confident in themselves and in their purposes. Teachers expect pupils to achieve; pupils know they are expected to achieve. Pupils and parents know that teachers are purposeful and competent – and are on their side.

   • The school's code of conduct is clear, and is understood to apply to the behaviours of teachers as well as pupils.

   • A climate is being established which supports an orderly and safe environment for pupils and for teachers and provides safeguards for those who are, or feel, unsafe.

5. Evidence of progress in relation to *pupils' capacity for learning* would include the following:

   • Pupils are developing a clear sense of their own achievements and of their own educational aspirations and needs.

   • Pupils are increasingly involved in the assessment of their own work; they are also involved in thinking, with their teachers, about relevant tasks and appropriate targets, and about how the decisions they make may affect their future.

- Pupils are gaining a sense of how the various learning experiences they are being offered 'add up' and achieve coherence.

- Pupils know what to do – whom to approach, whom to talk with – when they are experiencing a sense of failure or a lack of direction in their work or in their lives.

Progress is neither linear nor simply a matter of adopting a set of ready-made strategies. This study supports the view that progress is invariably uneven, and subject to occasional reversals. It also confirms the view that changing the practice of schooling necessarily involves changing the perceptions and understandings of teachers, pupils and parents. Progress, in discipline as in other aspects of schooling, is difficult to achieve because it is vulnerable both to the climate within the school and to the context without. The fact that the schools we have studied are, nevertheless, making progress under difficult circumstances is, we believe, grounds for optimism.

References

Apple, M. W. (1990) *Ideology and Curriculum* (second edition) (New York and London: Routledge).

Atkinson, R. (1989) 'Preface', in N. Jones (ed.) *School Management and Pupil Behaviour* (Lewes: Falmer), pp. ix–x.

Ball, S. J. (1987) *The Micro-Politics of the School: Towards a Theory of School Organisation* (London: Methuen).

Becker, H. S. (1953) 'The teacher in the authority system of the public school', reprinted in H.S. Becker (1970) *Sociological Work: Method and Substance* (New Brunswick: Transaction Books), pp. 151–63.

Brandt, G. L. (1986) *The Realization of Anti-Racist Teaching* (Lewes: Falmer).

Broadfoot, P., Grant, M., James, M., Nuttall, D. and Stierer, B. (1991) *Records of Achievement: Report of the National Evaluation of Extension Work in Pilot Schemes (PRAISE)* (London: Department of Education and Science/Welsh Office).

Broadfoot, P. and Nuttall, D. (1991) 'Review and conclusions' in P. Broadfoot, M. Grant, M. James, D. Nuttall and B. Stierer (1991) *Records of Achievement: Report of the National Evaluation of Extension Work in Pilot Schemes (PRAISE)* (London: Department of Education and Science/Welsh Office), pp. 65–79.

Carspecken, P. F. (1991) *Community Schooling and the Nature of Power: The Battle for Croxteth Comprehensive* (London: Routledge).

Cohen, P. and Bains, H. S. (1988) *Multi-Racist Britain* (London: Macmillan).

119

Connell, R. W., Ashenden, D. J., Kessler, S. and Dowsett, G. W. (1982) *Making the Difference* (Sydney: Allen and Unwin).

Cowie, H. and Rudduck, J. (1989) *School and Classroom Studies* (Volume 2 of Learning Together, Working Together) (London: BP Educational Service).

Department of Education and Science (1989) *Discipline in Schools: Report of the Committee of Enquiry* (The Elton Report) (London: HMSO).

Department of Employment (1991) *Recording Achievement and Planning Individual Development: Guidance on Summarising the Record and Completing the National Record of Achievement*, NRA3 (Sheffield: Employment Department).

Department of Employment/Department of Education and Science (1991) *National Record of Achievement* (London: Department of Employment/Department of Education and Science).

Docking, J. (1989) 'Elton's four questions: some general considerations', in N. Jones (ed.) *School Management and Pupil Behaviour* (Lewes: Falmer), pp. 6–26.

Furlong, R. J. (1991) 'Disaffected pupils: reconstructing the sociological perspective', *British Journal of Sociology of Education*, vol. 12, no. 3, pp. 293–307.

Galloway, D. (1990) *Pupil Welfare and Counselling* (London: Longman).

Galloway, D., Mortimore, P. and Tutt, N. (1989) 'Enquiry into discipline in schools', in N. Jones (ed.) *School Management and Pupil Behaviour* (Lewes: Falmer), pp. 93–104.

Gannaway, H. (1976) 'Making sense of school', reprinted in M. Hammersley and P. Woods (eds.) (1984) *Life in School: The Sociology of Pupil Culture* (Milton Keynes: Open University Press), pp. 191–203.

Gillborn, D. (1990) *'Race', Ethnicity and Education: Teaching and Learning in Multi-Ethnic Schools* (London: Unwin Hyman/Routledge).

Gillborn, D. (1991) 'Discipline and behaviour problems', in Rotherham Metropolitan Borough Council, *Working Together: Special Educational Needs in the Nineties* (Rotherham: Rotherham M.B.C.), pp. 28–32.

Gillborn, D. (1992) 'Racism and education: issues for research and practice' in S. Brown and S. Riddell (eds.) *Class, Race and Gender in Schools* (Edinburgh: Scottish Council for Research in Education), pp. 25–37.

Gillborn, D., Nixon, J. and Rudduck, J. (1989) 'Teachers' expectations and perceptions of discipline in ten inner-city comprehensive schools', in *Discipline in Schools: Report of the Committee of Enquiry* (The Elton Report) (London: HMSO), pp. 251–77.

Giroux, H. A. (1983) *Theory and Resistance in Education* (London: Heinemann Educational).

Gottlieb, R. S. (1979) 'Habermas and critical reflective emancipation', in T. F. Geraets (ed.) *Rationality Training* (Ottawa: University of Ottawa Press).

Gray, J. (1990) 'The quality of schooling: frameworks for judgment', *British Journal of Educational Studies*, vol. 38, no. 3, pp. 204–23.

Gray, J. and Jesson, D. (1990) 'The negotiation and construction of performance indicators: some principles, proposals and problems', *Evaluation and Research in Education*, vol. 4, no. 2, pp. 93–108.

Gray, J. and Sime, N. (1989) 'Findings from the national survey of teachers in England and Wales', in *Discipline in Schools: Report of the Committee of Enquiry* (The Elton Report) (London: HMSO), pp. 222–50.

Haldane, J. B .S. (1985) *On Being the Right Size, and Other Essays* (Oxford: Oxford University Press).

Hammersley, M. (1984) 'Staffroom news', in A. Hargreaves and P. Woods (eds.) (1984) *Classrooms and Staffrooms: The Sociology of Teachers and Teaching* (Milton Keynes: Open University Press), pp. 203–14.

Hargreaves, D. H. (1972) *Interpersonal Relations in Education* (London: Routledge and Kegan Paul).

Hargreaves, D. H. (1980) 'The occupational culture of teachers', in P. Woods (ed.) *Teacher Strategies: Explorations in the Sociology of the School* (London: Croom Helm), pp. 125–48.

Hargreaves, D. H. (1982) *The Challenge for the Comprehensive School* (London: Routledge and Kegan Paul).

Hargreaves, D. H. (1989) 'Introduction', in N. Jones (ed.) *School Management and Pupil Behaviour* (Lewes: Falmer), pp. 1–5.

Her Majesty's Inspectors (1989) *Education Observed 5: Good Behaviour and Discipline in Schools* (revised edition) (London: HMSO).

Jones, N. (1989) 'School discipline and the Elton Report', in N. Jones (ed.) *School Management and Pupil Behaviour* (Lewes: Falmer), pp. 244–65.

Keddy, P. A. (1989) *Competition* (London: Chapman and Hall).

Khanum, S. (1991) 'War talk', *New Statesman and Society*, 1 February.

Lipsitz, J. (1984) *Successful Schools for Young Adolescents* (New Brunswick: Transaction Books).

Mac an Ghaill, M. (1988) *Young, Gifted and Black: Student–Teacher Relations in the Schooling of Black Youth* (Milton Keynes: Open University Press).

Macdonald, I., Bhavnani, R., Khan, L. and John, G. (1989) *Murder in the Playground: The Burnage Report* (London: Longsight Press).

McGuff, I. (1990) 'Profiling and records of achievement', in R. Riding and S. Butterfield (eds) *Assessment and Examination in the Secondary School* (London: Routledge), pp. 104–31.

Modood, T. (1990a) 'British Asian muslims and the Rushdie affair', *Political Quarterly*, April, pp. 143–60.

Modood, T. (1990b) 'Catching up with Jessie Jackson: being oppressed and being somebody', *New Community*, vol. 17, no. 1, pp. 85–96.

Nash, I. (1991) 'Ministers are blamed for records failure', *Times Educational Supplement*, 1 March 1991, p. 4.

Nixon, J. (1992) *Evaluating the Whole Curriculum* (Milton Keynes: Open University Press).

Oakes, J. and Lipton, M. (1990) *Making the Best of Schools: A Handbook for Parents, Teachers and Policy Makers* (New York: Yale University Press).

Powell, A. G., Farrer, E. and Cohen, D. K. (1985) *The Shopping Mall High School* (Boston: Houghton Mifflin Company).

Ranger, C. (1988) *Ethnic Minority School Teachers* (London: Commission for Racial Equality).

Rizvi, F. and Kemmis, S. (1987) *Dilemmas of Reform: The Participation and Equity Program in Victorian Schools* (Deakin: Deakin Institute for Studies in Education).

Rudduck, J. (1991) *Innovation and Change: Developing Involvement and Understanding* (Milton Keynes: Open University Press).

Runnymede Trust, (1991) *Race and Immigration: Runnymede Trust Bulletin*, no. 244, April.

Shepherd, D. (1987) 'The accomplishment of divergence', *British Journal of Sociology of Education*, vol. 8, no. 3, pp. 263–76.

Smith, S. (1962) 'One of many', *Selected Poems* (London: Longmans).

Wehlage, G. G., Rutter, R. A., Smith, G. A., Lesko, N. and Fernandez, R. R. (1989) *Reducing the Risk: Schools as Communities of Support* (Lewes: Falmer).

Weindling, D. and Earley, P. (1987) *Secondary Headship: The First Years* (Windsor: NFER-Nelson).

Woods, P. (ed.) (1980a) *Pupil Strategies: Explorations in the Sociology of the School* (London: Croom Helm).

Woods, P. (ed.) (1980b) *Teacher Strategies: Explorations in the Sociology of the School* (London: Croom Helm).

Woods, P. (1983) *Sociology and the School: An Interactionist Viewpoint* (London: Routledge and Kegan Paul).

Woods, P. (1990) *The Happiest Days? How Pupils Cope with School* (Lewes: Falmer).

Wright, C. (1985) 'Learning environment or battleground?', *Multicultural Teaching*, vol. 4, no. 1, pp. 11–16.

Index

absenteeism
  see also attendance
  Burran School 49, 51–2
  Forest School 104
  Milner School 23
academic achievement
  Burran School 45, 49, 63, 90
  dimensions of discipline 110
  Elton Report 2
  Milner School 16–18, 23, 25, 26
  pupil population 10, 114–15
  Reid School 32
  Seaview School 65, 69–70, 72, 76–8, 83, 86, 87
  school concern 109
adult eduction
  community schools 47, 49, 92–5
  pupil relationship 96–8
Adult Education Centres 61
adult students *see* mature students
alienation 67
anti-racist committee 48, 58–61
apologies
  gender issues 57
  Seaview School policy 84
  teacher-pupil relationships 56
  work experience placements 61
Apple, M.W. 64, 119
arts
  Burran School 51–2
Asian communities 90, 96, 99–107
assemblies
  Milner School 18
assessment procedures
  curriculum profiles 71–3
  review process 75–8
  Seaview School 67–71, 111–12

Atkinson, R. 2, 119
attendance
  absenteesim 23, 49, 51–2, 104
  assessment structure 74
  Burran School 51–2, 97, 98
  Milner School 18, 21, 23
  parents' evenings 77–8
  pupils 114
attitudinal grids 73–5
authority
  community schools 90, 95
  management style 33
  teacher-pupil relationship 81
  traditional claims 65, 67
Bains, H.S. 107, 119
Baker, Kenneth 1
Ball, S.J. 43, 119
Becker, H.S. 33, 119
behaviour
  academic development 109
  Burran School 51, 54, 111
  discipline debate 9
  policy formation 35–7
Brandt, G.L. 99, 119
Broadfoot, P. 68, 119
Burnage enquiry 101, 104, 123
Burran School
  anti-racist policy 58–61
  anti-sexist behaviour 56–8
  behaviour sensitivity 111
  dialogue 5, 45–53, 111
  mature students 96–8
  pastoral system 55–6
  respect 89–93, 92–3, 99–100
  sanctions framework 54–5
  summary 62–4
  teacher-pupil relationships 53

cafe facilities
    community schools 92
Carspecken, P.F. 90, 119
census data 3–4
Class; *see* socio-economic environment
classrooms
    Burran School 54
    community schools 92
    dress policy 36
    mature students 97
    new teachers 40–2
    pupil engagement 80–1, 87
classwork 74
clothes *see* dress; uniform
Cohen, D.K. 9, 45, 123
Cohen, P. 107, 119
commitment 17, 24, 32, 52–3
communication 102–4
community
    adult participation 92–8
    Burran School 49
    'dimensions of discipline' 110
    'entrance tests' 40–1
    liaison officers 102–4
    research techniques 6
    teacher-pupil relationships 3, 5,
        56, 89, 111–13
community schools 28–43, 47–64
    adult access procedures 93
confrontation avoidance 52–3
Connell, R.W. 120
consistency 27–43, 107
    focusing concept 3, 110, 115
    standards 27–8
consultation, management style 33–5
contracts
    Burran School 54
counselling 55, 58, 61
coursework
    Milner School 21
    Seaview School 71
Cowie, H. 63, 120

creche facilities 92–3
crime 15, 65
Crown Prosecution Service 2
curriculum
    assessment policy 71
    planning 20–1, 23–4, 26, 52
    RoA role 68
Department of Education and Science
    discipline debate 68, 120
    Elton Report 2, 45, 103, 109, 120
Department of Employment 68, 120
detentions 14, 54, 83
dialogue 45–64
    anti-racist policy 58–61
    anti-sexist policy 56–8
    assessment structure 69–71, 73–5
    Burran School 47–53
    focusing concept 3, 5, 110–11, 115
    parents' evenings 77–8
    pastoral system 55–6
    pupil participation 68; *see* also
        engagement of pupils
    review process 76
    sanctions framework 54–5
    teacher-pupil relationships 53
'dimensions of discipline' 3, 110
disabled groups 96
discipline
    perspectives 1–8, 110–17
disruption
    discipline debate 9, 54, 111
    low level 2
    'race' issues 58–61
Docking, J. 1, 2, 120
dress 36, 58–9
drug taking problem 46–7
Earley, P. 31, 33, 124
education
    community schools 90–3
    community view 5
    holistic approach 17–18, 22
    institution view 1, 3

pupil engagement 65–88
    state funding 88
Education Reform Act 12
Educational Welfare Officers 29
Elton Committee of Enquiry (1988) 1
Elton Report (1989) 2, 45, 103, 109
empowerment of pupils 66–7
engagement of pupils 65–88
    assessment structure 67–71
    attitudinal grids 73–5
    focusing concept 3, 6, 110–11, 115
    profiles 71–3
    pupils 65–7
    review process 75–8
    sanctions 83–7
    teacher-pupil relationships 78–82
English teaching 50
entry process 50–1
equal opportunities *see* gender issues;
    racism
ERA *see* Education Reform Act
ethnic composition
    anti-racist measures 58–61
    dialogue 45–6
    pupil populations 5, 15–16, 48
    school-community relationship
        89–90, 96, 99–100, 102–4, 106–8
EWOs *see* Educational Welfare Officers
examinations 67, 71, 91, 97–8
exclusions 38, 54–5, 60–1, 84
expectations 9–26
    Burran School 49
    focusing concept 3, 6, 110–11, 115
    Milner School 9–10, 14–17, 23–5
    pupil engagement 78–9
    Reid School 35
explanations
    assessment structure 69–71
family structure
    academic achievement 114
    inner city schools 4, 90
Farrer, E. 9, 45, 123

flexibility debate 27, 35
Forest School
    communication 102–4
    community respect 89, 101–2,
    104–7
    ethnic composition 100–1
form teachers
    pupil engagement 86–7
    review process 75–8
funding
    community schools 92
    state education 88, 103
Furlong, R.J. 46, 63–4, 120
Galloway, D. 2, 18, 109, 120
Gannaway, H. 85, 120
GCSE *see* General Certificate of
    Secondary Education
gender issues
    anti-sexist policy 22, 36, 48, 56–8
    mature students 97
    teacher professionalism 16–17
General Certificate of Secondary
    Education 12, 71
Gillborn, D. 2, 33, 37, 75, 86, 99, 102,
    121
Giroux, H.A. 46, 121
Gottlieb, R.S. 45, 121
governors
    community schools 91, 98
    permanent exclusions 55
Gray, J. 2, 63, 121
Gulf War 104–7
Haldane, J.B.S. 1, 122
Hammersley, M. 75, 122
harassment
    counter-measures 22, 47–8, 56–61
    LEA guidelines 47
Hargreaves, D.H. 2, 20, 37, 64, 109,
    122
headteachers
    Burran School 48–50, 54
    community schools 91, 95

Forest School 100–1
language debate 101–2
managerial style 33
Milner School 11–13, 13–14
parents' evenings 77–8
peer support policy 38
permanent exclusions 54–5
pupil empowerment 66–7
Reid School 28, 30–1, 33–5, 38–9, 40, 43
research techniques 6
sanctions debate 83–5
school philosophy 113
work experience placements 61
health 46, 51
Her Majesty's Inspectors 6, 27, 36, 122
HMI see Her Majesty's Inspectors
homework 18, 21, 50
Hussein, Saddam
    see Saddam Hussein
in-service education and training 30, 34, 42
Indian subcontinent
    migration 100
information technology 50
INSET see In-service education and training
interview techniques
    explanation 5–6
'issue groups'
    Reid School 33–5
Jesson, D. 63, 121
job markets 65–6
    community schools 92
    pupils 53
Jones, N. 2, 110, 122
Keddy, P.A. 1, 122
Kemmis, S. 45, 123
Khanum, S. 104, 122
language factors
    of critique 63

mother tongue issues 101–4
    refugees 95
large families see family structure
leadership see headteachers
    HMI report 27
LEAs see local education authorities
libraries 34
Lipsitz, J. 10, 122
LMS see Local Management of Schools
local education authorities 11, 46–9, 91, 98, 103
Local Management of Schools 12
Mac an Ghaill, M. 102, 123
Macdonald, I. 101, 104, 123
McGuff, I. 65, 123
'maintenance' groups
    Reid School 34, 36
management systems
    Burran School 48
    community schools 94
    democratic style 33
    discipline structure 110, 113, 115
    Forest School 101
    Gulf War 106
    Milner School 13–14, 17
    peer support 38–9
    Reid School 28, 30
    sanctions debate 84
    Seaview School 85
    teacher relationship 5
Manchester 104
mature students
    community schools 47, 49, 92–5
    pupil relationship 96–8
media 32, 88
    school violence reports 1–2
Milner School
    conclusions 26
    dynamics 10–13
    expectations 4, 9–10, 14–17, 111
    learning 17–22

transition period 22–5
Modood, T. 105, 123
morale
    Forest School 100–1
    Reid School 30–1
    teachers 2, 9, 37–42
mosques 105
motivation
    pupils 23, 64, 65–7, 69, 98
    school concern 3, 9, 109, 113
multicultural communities
    Burran School 90, 95–6
    Forest School 101, 104
    Milner School 11
    Reid School 34
name-calling 22, 57, 60
Nash, I. 68, 123
National Curriculum 12, 50
National Front 90, 105
National Record of Achievement 68
negotiation *see* dialogue
newsletters
    language debate 103
Nixon, J. 2, 26, 121, 123
Oakes, J. 114, 123
on-call system
    Reid School 38–9
on-report system
    Burran School 54
    Seaview School PPS policy 86
one-parent families *see* family
    structure
outreach centres 91, 95
parents
    assessment structure 75–8, 88
    Burran School 49–54, 94–5
    community schools 29, 91, 93–4,
    98
    Forest School 102–4
    mature students 49
    Milner School 18, 21–2
    pupil motivation 115

research techniques 6
review process 77–8
school participation 46–8, 112–13
teacher-pupil relationships 56
work experience placements 61
Parents' Group
    Burran School 50, 59
participation
    community schools 93–6, 98
    pupils 24 *see* also dialogue;
        engagement
    teachers 30–42, 75–8, 82–7, 111,
        112–13, 115–6
pastoral system
    Burran School 48–9, 55–6
    Milner School 11, 17–22
    parents' evenings 77–8
    Seaview School 85
peer support policy 37–42, 107, 111
Personal Progress Support policy 86
Pilot Records of Achievement in
    Schools Evaluation 68
playgrounds 52
police 85, 105–7
policy formation
    Reid School 28, 33–7
Powell, A.G. 9, 45, 123
PPS policy *see* Personal Progress
    Support policy
PRAISE *see* Pilot Records of
    Achievement in Schools
    Evaluation
profiles
    assessment structure 71–3
punctuality
    assessment structure 74
    Milner School 21, 23
    Seaview School 84
Punjabi language 100, 102–3
pupils
    Asian 100–107
    assessment 67–75

dialogue development 45–7
dimensions of discipline 110
disaffection 9, 46, 65, 87, 96
dress 58–9
expectations 23, 32, 41, 53, 65, 114
Forest School 100–1
gender issues 56–8
Gulf War 104–7
mature students 96–8
motivation 3, 9, 15–16, 23–4, 98
negotiation policy 79–80
pastoral care 21–2
policy formation 113, 116–17
potential 13, 25
'race' issues 16–17, 22, 52, 58–61
Reid School 28–9, 40–1
research techniques 6
review process 75–8
sanctions 83–7
school perspective 114–15
Seaview School 65–76, 85–8
work experience placements 61
community schools 49, 112
mature students 97
racism *see also* pupils and teachers:
'race' issues
community schools 90, 95–6,
101–2
counter-measures 52, 58–61,
101–2, 104–7
Gulf War 105–7
Ranger, C. 104, 123
Record of Achievement
parent-pupil relationship 81–2
purpose 67–9, 72, 74
review process 76–7
recruitment
Milner School 11
Reid School 40–1
Seaview School 88
refugees
community schools 95

Reid School
behaviour 35–7
conclusions 42–3
consistency 28–31
peer support 37–42
policy formation 4, 33–5, 111
value system 31–3
Reid Values Statement 31–6, 42
religious festivals 104
reports 69, 70, 72, 103
see also on-report system
research techniques
outline 5–7
respect 89–108
Burran School 49, 61
communication 102–4
community schools 92–3, 98,
100–1
development 89–90
equal value 101–2
focusing concept 3, 110, 116
Forest School 101–2, 104–8
gender issues 57–8
learning 90–1
mature students 96–8
Milner School 10, 18
multicultural communities 101–2
parent-teacher relationship 94–5
participation 93–6, 98–9
principles and practice 104–7
pupil motivation 99–100, 115
restraint
discipline debate 9
review process
assessment structure 75–8
revision 51
reward systems 18–19
Rizvi, F. 45, 123
RoA *see* Record of Achievement
Rudduck, J. 2, 63, 68, 120, 121, 124
Runnymede Trust 105, 124
Saddam Hussein 105–6

sanctions
    Burran School 54–5
    Seaview School 83–7
schools
    community relationship 5, 11,
        28–9, 31, 32, 40–1, 47–9, 52–3, 65–6,
        88, 89–108, 110, 113, 114
    description 3–5
    dimensions of discipline 110
Seaview School
    assessment structures 71–5
    conclusions 87–8
    pupil engagement 5, 65–7, 111–12
    review process 75–8
    sanctions 83–7
    teacher-pupil relationships 78–82
security 52
self-discipline 10
self-reliance 53
sexism 56–8
    see also gender issues
Shepherd, D 99, 124
Sime, N. 2, 121
single parent families see family
    structure
sixth-form colleges 98
Smith, S. 46, 124
social class structure
    community respect 89–90
    pupil populations 4–5, 28–9, 48, 66
socio-economic environment
    Burran School 48, 53, 90–1
    community schools 96
    dialogue 45–6
    Forest School 100–1
    Milner School 14–15
    pupil populations 3–4, 109, 114
    Reid School 28–9
    Seaview School 65–6
Special Needs Support departments
    Seaview School 87–8
sport 51–2

stability
    teachers 11–12
staff meetings
    community schools 93, 101
    Reid School 30–1, 38
standards
    consistency 27–8
Statement of Partnership
    Burran School 50–1
sub-cultures
    Burran School 49, 52, 58–60
    dialogue 62
support see peer support
tale-telling
    Burran School 59–60
teacher-pupil relationship
    assessment 67–73
    Burran School 55–6, 59, 63
    consistency debate 27
    development 78–82
    dialogue 45–6, 53, 113
    Forest School 102, 105–6, 107
    language debate 101–2
    Milner School 16, 17–25, 18–20
    Reid School 40–2
    Seaview School 65–7, 78–85
teachers
    black 104
    Burran School 52–3
    community involvement 92–3
    Community liaison 102–4
    dimensions of discipline 110
    expectations 10, 23
    fatigue 30–1
    Forest School 100–1
    gender issues 36, 56–8
    home-liaison 94
    Milner School 11
    morale 2, 5, 9
    peer support 37–42
    professional identity 16–17, 78–82
    pupil exploitation 53

race' issues 11–12, 15–16, 59–61, 99–100, 101–7
Reid School 28–9, 31–5, 36
research techniques 6
review process 75–8
sanctions 83–7
values 27–43
Technical and Vocational Education Initiative 12, 71
timetables
community schools 92
on-call system 38–9
Reid School 30
training see in-service education and training
training days
pupil engagement 67
Reid School 32
Seaview School 84
truancy 51 see also absenteeism
tutorial system
Milner School 17–18, 21, 26
pastoral care 22, 55
Seaview School 75–8, 86–7
TVEI see Technical and Vocational Education Initiative
unemployment
community schools 90
parents 49
pupil motivation 15, 65
schools profile 109
uniform 50, 59

Urdu language 100
vacations 51
values
Burran School 49, 63–4
Milner School 14–17, 20, 22
Reid School 31–5, 42
school staff 27-43
violence 2
Burran School 46–7, 52, 61, 92
Elton Report 1–2
Reid School 28, 35
Forest School 106
Wehlage, G.G. 114, 124
Weindling, D. 31, 33, 124
'White flight' 100
whole-school organisation
community schools 94
dialogue 45
discipline structure 112–14, 116
Forest School 107
planning 17, 26
policy formation 2, 4–5
Reid School 33–5
Woods, P. 27, 40, 85, 124
work experience placements 61
Wright, C. 102, 124
year groups
Burran School 51, 55–6
youth clubs
community schools 92
Youth Workers 61

Printed in the United Kingdom for HMSO.
Dd.0295706, 8/92, C20, 3396/4, 5673, 219840.